EDWARD G. ROBINSON

EDWARD G. ROBINSON

A Pyramid Illustrated History of the Movies

by
FOSTER HIRSCH

General Editor: TED SENNETT

PUBLICATIONS
NEW YORK

**EDWARD G. ROBINSON
A Pyramid Illustrated History of the Movies**

Copyright © 1975 by Pyramid Communications, Inc.
All rights reserved. No part of this book may be reproduced in any form or by any electronic or mechanical means including information storage and retrieval systems without permission in writing from the Publisher, except by a reviewer who may quote brief passages in a review.

Pyramid edition published February 1975

ISBN 0-515-03642-0

Library of Congress Catalog Card Number: 75-613

Printed In the United States of America

Pyramid Books are published by Pyramid Communications, Inc. Its trademarks, consisting of the word "Pyramid" and the portrayal of a pyramid, are registered in the United States Patent Office.

Pyramid Communications, Inc., 919 Third Avenue, New York, N.Y. 10022

CONDITIONS OF SALE

"Any sale, lease, transfer or circulation of this book by way of trade or in quantites of more than one copy, without the original cover bound thereon, will be construed by the Publisher as evidence that the parties to such transaction have illegal possession of the book, and will subject them to claim by the Publisher and prosecution under the law."

(graphic design by anthony basile)

ACKNOWLEDGMENTS

Patrick Sheehan and Joe Balian at the Library of Congress; the staff at the Lincoln Center Library of Performing Arts; Charles Silver at the Museum of Modern Art Film Study Center; Ted Sennett.

Photographs: Jerry Vermilye, The Memory Shop, Cinemabilia, Movie Star News, Columbia Pictures.

CONTENTS

Introduction: The Boss 11
The Stage Years 18
Robinson in the Thirties: Little Caesar and Others 27
Robinson in the Forties: Ehrlich to Rocco 64
Robinson in the Fifties: Keeping Busy in a Lean Time 106
The Last Years 122
Bibliography 143
The Films of Edward G. Robinson 145
Index 155

INTRODUCTION: THE BOSS

"The squat frame, the moon-face, the rubbery lips that were ever consuming a $1 cigar, the metallic voice that landed like a tattoo of blows"*—Edward G. Robinson was the least likely of movie stars. He was short and swarthy and hefty. His eyes were sad and puffy. His mouth drooped. With age, his deeply lined face sagged and he looked more and more dyspeptic.

His voice, too, was decidedly unheroic. Snarling and gravelly, it remained unmistakably Lower East Side despite the overlay of actor's training. With its sharp, cutting edge, the voice matched the curled lip and the features that seemed to arrange themselves in a perpetual sneer.

Nature surely intended him to be a supporting actor, but Robinson was that rare case, a character actor who became a star. And he was that even more singular phenomenon —a star who *remained* a star for forty years. In the fifties and sixties, Robinson was not given the kind of role in the kind of movie that had sustained him for almost twenty years after the success of *Little Caesar*. But he worked almost continuously, and he always got prominent billing. Unlike many of the actors who started in early sound films, Robinson was active right up to his death. In some of his later parts, in the sixties, he played old-time gangsters whose lingo and manner of dress had nostalgic echoes, but Robinson was never reduced to being a museum piece. For forty years he held his own.

Crusty, ethnic, plain, Robinson was one of the sound film's first antiheroes. Both on screen and off, he was the scrappy little guy who made it despite the odds. Born Emanuel Goldenberg in Bucharest, Romania, in 1893, Robinson was the poor Jewish immigrant who made something of himself; he was the funny-looking kid from the Lower East Side who studied hard to become a professional. Even though he often played twisted, anti-social characters, audiences warmed to Robinson; they responded to his energy and determination, to his brash, staccato style. "I can't give you much face value," Robinson told producers early in his career, "but I can give you stage value." An actor who humanized villains and misfits, Robinson had dynamic presence, and he was the inevitable center of attention in almost all of his movies.

In a fiercely competitive industry

Time, February 5, 1973.

that reveres youth and beauty, Robinson's unheroic looks proved to be an asset. Unlike romantic leading men whose careers are threatened by the first signs of age, Robinson didn't have to worry about creases and wrinkles and weight—he had never looked young and trim in the first place. The homeliness did present problems of type-casting, however; Robinson could always get work, but too often it turned out to be the same kind of work. Though he played a variety of roles, Robinson, in fact, will always be identified with the character he made an American archetype, the ambitious gangster whose diseased conception of the American dream offered an upside-down Horatio Alger success story. Robinson was almost too effective as Little Caesar, and as a result audiences and producers never fully accepted him in other than an urban crime context. When the actor fought his studio for the chance to expand his image, when he played a noble scientist or a philosophical farmer, when, later in his career, he played an assortment of professors and lawyers, Robinson earned favorable reviews, but his nongangster roles were often considered stunts and temporary departures.

Short and overweight, the actor was inescapably typecast: he played comic gangsters, gangsters dressed up as monks, retired and fallen gangsters, gangsters on the comeback trail, policemen who *pretended* to be gangsters, gangsters gone straight, businessmen who used the ethics of the gang. Whether he was cop or hood, private investigator or kingpin mobster, Robinson almost always operated in a criminal world; even if he didn't run with the pack, it was as if he knew in his bones the code of the gang.

"I don't want to be remembered as a crook," Robinson grumbled periodically. But he realized that he had his greatest impact playing criminals: "Some people have youth. Some people have beauty. I have menace. People would go to see me in the movies so they could hate me."* Robinson protested from time to time, but he was a shrewd businessman, and he participated in the unflattering casting. Capitalizing on a face and physique that conveyed menace, Robinson turned himself into one of Hollywood's ultimate tough guys. In creating a series of characters who snarled and slugged their way to power, Robinson had only two peers: James Cagney and Humphrey Bogart.

Robinson's big roles were characters determined to take over the

*Interview with Glen Hicks, *National Enquirer*, June 10, 1969.

town. Bosses, con men, investigators, the Robinson kingpins were the top men in town, the men who made it not by luck or charm or inheritance but by hard work and shrewd manipulation. Unlike Cagney's or Bogart's characters, Robinson's brash, swaggering bosses did not devastate women. Robinson lacked the kind of lopsided looks that had romantic allure. On screen, the actor was often womanless. Rarely was he even a patriarchal figure; he was a solitary leader of men rather than head of a family. Often playing a sexual misfit, Robinson enjoyed only some tentative understandings with mistresses and only a few times was he allowed the comforts of a wife and family. The typical Robinson boss was a loner—distrustful, guarded, more attached to men than to women. The underlying sexual maladjustment added novel twists to the Robinson outlaws—his were never simply conventional villains. Sexually abstinent, the archetypal Robinson gangster was zealously devoted to his work, and he rose higher than others because he was more single-minded, sublimating his thwarted sexual drive into an obsessive quest for power.

Robinson's "heroes" were often grotesques. Striving for money and power in underhanded ways, they cut themselves off from the moral norm. They made their own laws, and their isolation from any sort of community made them dangerous.

Robinson savored the opportunities his sinister, psychotic characters offered, but his publicity always stressed the fact that he was only acting. Robinson appreciated the acclaim he received for playing Little Caesar, but he wanted his public to understand that in fact he was not simply playing himself. In 1931 Sidney Skolsky assured movie fans that Robinson "has never met Al Capone. He does not know and never did mix with the types who brought him national fame. He's a good actor, that's all."* Right after *Little Caesar*, newspaper items informed moviegoers that "the hardest-boiled man in the movies is a soft-spoken little master of arts from Columbia University and a graduate of the New York Theater Guild . . . There's probably no actor alive who can portray concentrated cruelty, unlimited ruthlessness, bottled venom and bottomless hatred as can this mild-voiced, wide-mouthed, sparkling-eyed little Romanian. And he's gentle, kindly, intellectual and mild."

To counter the tough movie image, to prove to audiences that he was very different from the bosses he played, Robinson was always eager to publicize himself as an art collector: "Little Caesar is far more

The New Movie Magazine, December 1931.

interested in works of art than in bullets, in books rather than bravado."** Robinson continued to act partly because he always needed money to add to his renowned collection. "My paintings cannot be valued in dollars," he said. "They cost all the years of my life . . . Late at night, when the house is quiet, when the last guest has gone, I go into my living room and sit down among these quiet friends, and we study each other very gravely, and I hope with mutual pleasure."***

In real life a cultivated gentleman, a lover of paintings, books and music, a philanthropist and good citizen, Robinson made his reputation playing crazed tyrants. A shrewd craftsman, a practical businessman, Robinson consciously created a vivid and marketable movie image.

**Jim Tully, *New York Herald Tribune*, November 29, 1936.
***Quoted in *Newsweek*, April 16, 1973.

THE STAGE YEARS

Edward G. Robinson has one of the steadiest and most conscientious track records in Hollywood history, but in his early days, when he trained for the stage at the American Academy of Dramatic Arts, he had no thought of working in movies. As a child of nine, he had left his native Romania to make his way in the "new world," eventually establishing himself as a stage actor. Like many New York actors, Robinson looked down on motion pictures. He went to California at the height of his stage fame for only one reason—money.

In the theater, in the late teens and throughout the twenties, Robinson performed in a variety of plays. As active on Broadway as he was to be in Hollywood for over forty years, Robinson moved restlessly between popular entertainments and avant garde experiments.* He appeared with Jacob Ben-Ami in English adaptations of Yiddish plays; he supported Ethel Barrymore in a dreadful costume drama. Between engagements with the Theater Guild, he was featured in mysteries, melodramas, a college comedy, and a drawing-room comedy in which he had an infrequent opportunity to play an Anglo-Saxon. His ethnic features usually won him foreign parts. In his first Broadway show, a potboiler called *Under Fire* (1915), Robinson played what he later called a sort of "League of Nations": a Belgian, a Frenchman, a German, and a cockney Englishman. In *The Deluge*, he played a Swede; in *The Pawn*, a Filipino; in *The Little Teacher*, a French-Canadian. He seldom had a straight part, and though he was young at the time, he was hardly ever the juvenile. Robinson played more Jews on stage in the twenties than he ever played in movies. On film, Robinson was rarely conspicuously Jewish; by the end of the twenties, after having appeared in a number of folk tales and ethnic comedies, he was close to being typed as a Yiddish actor.

In the mid-twenties, Robinson acted with The Theater Guild in prestigious and often difficult foreign and American plays. The Guild assigned him to dark, twisted characters, murderers and misfits, but they entrusted him with roles in

---

*He appeared in one silent movie, *The Bright Shawl* (1923), with Richard Barthelmess, Dorothy Gish, William Powell and Mary Astor.

THE BRIGHT SHAWL (1923). With Mary Astor, Margaret Seddon, Luis Alberni, and André de Beranger

light comedies as well. He moved from Dostoyevsky's sinister epileptic Smerdiakov to a low-comedy Caesar in Shaw's *Androcles and the Lion*, from a burlesque Jewish peddler in Franz Werfel's *Goat Song* to a crisp Yankee lawyer in Sidney Howard's *Ned McCobb's Daughter*. In Pirandello's *Right You Are*, Robinson had the kind of tricky, double-edged role that he often played in films: he was a man who feigns madness, and who is deranged or sane as the occasion demanded. In Werfel's historical pageant, *Juarez and Maximilian*, Robinson was even given the chance to be conventionally heroic.

Robinson worked with the leading actors and directors: the Lunts, Pauline Lord, Joseph Schildkraut, Arthur Hopkins, Komisarjevsky, George Arliss. He was always well reviewed, especially by Alexander Woollcott, who wrote of his Caesar in *Androcles:* "The role comes suddenly, surprisingly, magnificently to life for the first time, played with great gusto by that capital actor, Edward G. Robinson. The whole episode, behind the imperial box at the Coliseum, is managed with a new zest and a new imagination."*

The Guild's pay scale was modest, however, and Robinson, ever a no-nonsense businessman, did not renew his contract. After he left the Guild, Robinson became a Broadway star, but he appeared in commercial claptrap. *The Man with Red Hair* (1928) was the first play in which the actor was starred. Sporting a flaming red wig, Robinson played a maniacal masochist. "He is oily, sinister; he snarls, pants, dances with glee as he feels the edges of his knives," wrote Arthur Ruhl in the *New York Herald Tribune* (November 9, 1928). In the *New York Sun*, Stephen Rathburn thought Robinson was fine "in his more passive scenes, largely through the cadences of his gentle, insinuating, horribly menacing voice. Unfortunately, long before

The New York World, November 24, 1923.

the climax, he breaks into the shrill ravings of the traditional stage lunatic. The most important fact is that Robinson has become a star . . . he proves in his present characterization that he is without peer . . . his only rival in his particular field is Lon Chaney."

In *The Kibitzer*, which Robinson co-authored with Jo Swerling (later a top screen writer), the actor played the owner of an Amsterdam Avenue cigar store. The show was designed as a star vehicle, and Robinson loved doing a part that was both comic and sentimental. He admitted that *The Kibitzer* was "a simple-minded ethnic play," but he thought it would be his insurance policy for years. The crash and the advent of the talkies, however, kept the show from becoming the audience favorite Robinson thought it would be.

Earlier in 1928, after a first version of *The Kibitzer* had failed, Robinson appeared in *The Racket*. The play was an ordinary crime melodrama, but Robinson's performance as a gangster modeled on Al Capone caught the attention of movie producers when the show was on tour in Los Angeles. Robinson approached his first gangster role reluctantly because "it was against theatrical precedent to create a character devoid of audience sympathy. I risked my career to dramatize for the public the

In one of his early stage appearances in the Yiddish theatre

THE HOLE IN THE WALL (1929). With Claudette Colbert

menace that confronted it."*
Robinson thoroughly disliked the part: "In order to play a part, you must have some kind of identification with the role; I had little understanding of larceny and murder. I would be forced to invent the gangster since I had no yardstick by which to create him."** Robinson's "invented" gangster, of course, changed his life.

Prodded by Hollywood producers, Robinson accepted several movie offers in 1929 and 1930, even though he thought of himself as a stage actor who was hiring himself out to movies on the sly. Robinson eagerly returned to New York in 1930, to appear in *Mr. Samuel*, based on a popular French play that was rewritten expressly for him. For his work as a Jewish captain of industry, he received some ungenerous reviews. Arthur Pollack, in the *Brooklyn Eagle*, complained that Robinson was "too intent on proving himself a virtuoso to bring reality to his role; he is a well-equipped actor more in love with his equipment than with the character allotted him." Robinson's star vehicle closed in a week, and the star was disgusted: "I thought to myself: 'What's all this about being true to the theater? Who's true to me? Eighteen years of acting and nobody will come to see me after the first week. What am I being true to?' "*** Concluding that theatergoers had no loyalty to him, Robinson decided to move to Hollywood and become a full-time movie actor, a fate he had avoided for as long as he could.

Robinson's films before *Little Caesar* are all undistinguished. Of his first talkie, a society comedy called *The Hole in the Wall* (1929), Robinson says it was "the stinker of all time." He had a meaty role in *A Lady to Love* (1930) (based on Sidney Howard's *They Knew What They Wanted*) as an old Italian farmer who sends for a mail-order bride. This was one of the few romantic and sentimental characters that Robinson would ever play, and his performance was animated. (Ten years later, Charles Laughton, also in an expansive mood, played the character opposite Carole Lombard; this time, the filmmakers kept Howard's original title.) *A Lady to Love* was the first of Robinson's triangle romance pictures in which the swarthy, jowly actor loses the leading lady to a handsome juvenile. Though Robinson performed with flair, the film was ruined by a wildly miscast Vilma

---

*Robinson, *The New York World-Telegram*, October 13, 1937.
**Edward G. Robinson, with Leonard Spigelgass, *All My Yesterdays* (New York: Hawthorn, 1973), p. 98

***Interview with Murray Schumach, *The New York Times*, February 5, 1956.

Banky. In his autobiography, Robinson reports, "It did not take long to realize that Miss Banky was seriously out of her depth. The glorious creature, playing a mail-order bride, complete with marcelled hair and a custom-made housedress and still the shimmering beauty she was with Ronald Colman in so many silent films, was seized with stage fright and inability."*

*Robinson, *All My Yesterdays*, p. 104.

In his other films before *Little Caesar*, Robinson was already typecast as a gangster. In *Night Ride* (1929), he's mobster Tony Garotta. In *Outside the Law* (1930), he's gang leader Cobra Collins. In *East is West* (1930), he plays Charlie Yong, known as the chop suey king. In these films, Robinson was accused of mugging; trapped in penny-dreadful parts, the actor overdid it, swooping down on his roles with exaggerated gusto. But in *The*

A LADY TO LOVE (1930). With Vilma Banky and Robert Ames

OUTSIDE THE LAW (1930). With Mary Nolan and Owen Moore

Widow from Chicago (1930), his star presence is unmistakable. Fitting snugly into the classic night world milieu of the thirties gangster cycle, Robinson plays a rackets warlord who runs a nightclub and who wants to take over the town. In a variation on the classic revenge motif, the heroine (Alice White) masquerades as a gunman's widow in order to get the gangster who killed her brother. Robinson, of course, is her antagonist. After much effort, the "widow" traps him, and in what was to become Robinson's typical movie fate, he ends up without woman or status.

For all its shortcomings (Alice White's performance is pitiful), the film offers some interesting variations on role-playing themes; masquerade is crucial to the way of the underworld here as it is in later and more refined crime stories. And Robinson plays with the authority that was to make his reputation in

EAST IS WEST (1930). With Charles Middleton

Hollywood. For moviegoers at the time, *Little Caesar* should have come as no surprise: the sneer, the commanding, snarling voice, the sharply pointed gestures, the caginess with women, the stinging sarcasm, the single-minded lust for power, even the cigar, are all here in Robinson's mature and beautifully crafted performance. In this first of his full-scale movie gangsters with a Napoleon complex, the Robinson characterization is already in high gear.

ROBINSON IN THE THIRTIES: LITTLE CAESAR AND OTHERS

Gangsters were popular from the very beginning of sound films, but none of the early gangsters had the impact of Caesar Enrico Bandello. Moving through the Chicago gang world as if this was the first time movies had shown what happened behind the mobs' closed doors, *Little Caesar* had the feel of an original. Along with *The Public Enemy* and *Scarface*, Mervyn LeRoy's film established the conventions of a genre as uniquely American as the Western.

The timing was right: in the early thirties, America was suffering from the combined blows of the Depression and Prohibition. It was difficult to make money in honest ways; Prohibition encouraged a flourishing underworld, and the gangster, who turned the Horatio Alger myth upside-down, became a temporary hero for a time in the nation's history when traditional values had conspicuously failed.

As it documents the meteoric rise and precipitous fall of a zealous mobster anxious to make good in the Chicago underworld, *Little Caesar* set a pattern for movie stories about gangsters. Carefully itemizing the mob's code, the film has an archetypal, simplified structure. Rico's acquisition of power is detailed step by step, almost as a case study of how to succeed as a criminal. Initially an outsider, dissatisfied with small-time jobs, Rico (called Little Caesar) has strong success drives. A boy from the sticks, he moves to the big city and dedicates himself to making good as conscientiously as any professional with a fierce will to achieve. Rico ingratiates himself with a gang. Anxious to please, he follows orders, but he's shrewd enough not to follow every order. On his first team job, robbing a nightclub on New Year's Eve, he shoots to kill when he's been warned not to. In his first act of bravado, he fires at, and hits, the city's crime commissioner.

Soon, having insinuated himself into the higher brackets of the mob, he edges out his immediate boss. Because he devotes himself to his work with such monastic dedication, Rico rises swiftly. He shuns distractions: he doesn't drink (it's only after he's washed up that he begins to), and he doesn't go with women.

Little Caesar permits himself to have feelings only for his hometown friend Joe (Douglas Fairbanks, Jr.), and it's those feelings that contribute to his downfall. He assumes toward Joe a brotherly protectiveness. He wants the kid to follow him into crime rather than to pursue a

LITTLE CAESAR (1930). A confrontation with the mob

dancing career ("That's woman's stuff," Rico sneers). His fiercest enemy is Joe's dancing partner, Olga Stassoff (Glenda Farrell); in contrast to the promise of big money that Rico uses to entice his friend, Olga offers Joe a safe career and domestic contentment.

Rico tries desperately to keep the kid from going soft. When Joe begins to withdraw into the straight world, Rico even protects him from the gang's attempts at retaliation. Rico's fondness for Joe (which is perhaps unconsciously homosexual) is his fatal flaw: it makes him what he cannot afford to be in his line of work—soft and human.

As quickly as he took over, Little Caesar plummets to a Bowery-like flop house. Abstemious, asexual Rico, stripped of power, is transformed into a cringing, whimpering wino who's trapped by one final appeal to his vanity from the cop who's wanted to nab him from the beginning. The erstwhile kingpin mobster dies in the gutter, shot down behind a billboard advertising the dancing team of Joe Masera and Olga Stassoff. His final words—"Mother of Mercy, is this the end of Rico?,"—are part of movie lore.

Robinson's performance is, of course, the film's centerpiece. Though contemporary critics praised him for playing a gangster realistically, Robinson, in fact, is highly mannered. The actor's theatrical heightening is present in the emphatic gestures, the stentorian tones, the exaggerated movement. In *Little Caesar*, and throughout most of the thirties, Robinson was not a subtle actor; with broad, occasionally garish strokes, he points up his character's foolish vanity, brute determination, and remarkable naïveté. Emphasizing the character's neurotic maladjustments, Robinson endows the role with some Freudian kinks that are only dimly present in W.R. Burnett's original novel.

Step by step, Robinson shows us what his character is thinking; though the kind of signaling he employs is overly emphatic and though he sometimes plays down to his character, commenting from above on Rico's gullibility and stupidity, his characterization is surprisingly

LITTLE CAESAR (1930). A holdup. With George E. Stone (at right)

LITTLE CAESAR (1930). Rico's final shoot-out

complex. Robinson's hood isn't simply a two-dimensional Machiavelli; he's tough, all right, ruthless when he has to be—"a cold, ignorant, merciless killer," wrote *The New York Times* in 1931—but he's a big kid too, proudly showing off his gaudy new house and admiring himself in a mirror when he's dressed up in a tuxedo.

Without overdoing it, Robinson manages to elicit our sympathy for his antisocial, borderline psychopath. Beneath the operatic flourish, the bravado, the swagger, there are hints of a character who resembles the rest of us. Robinson always managed to give his villains some human dimension.

Little Caesar is far from the actor's best work, but his vigorous, staccato delivery had style, and this stage actor with a most unprepossessing appearance introduced a new kind of rebel hero to Depression-era movies. Robinson doesn't make Little Caesar glamorous, but he does bring to the character a decidedly heroic presence. He gives Rico stature. He makes him a man to contend with. Whatever sympathy the film may finally extend to Rico, though, it presents the syndicate as a singularly ruthless group: far from being a subversive film in which crime is glamorized, *Little Caesar* depicts the underworld as bleak and infested. The most powerful scenes in the picture are, in fact, those of Rico's decline: crime is very emphatically punished.

Because of Robinson, however, the criminal has more energy than the straight people. Little Caesar is more beguiling than the woman who claims Joe, for instance, and he is even more balanced than the high-strung law enforcement officer who pursues him with such diabolical glee. If the world of the criminal is cutthroat and terrifyingly uncertain, the social world outside his domain is either anemic or unconsciously warped.

Little Caesar is a dark movie, its settings the grim rooms hidden behind blinking neon lights; it presents an unromantic view of the American big city as fatally corrupt. In public statements about the film (and about the thirties gangster cycle in general), Robinson always emphasized social value: "The gangster pictures didn't bolster the depiction of violence or influence youth to violent acts after seeing them. Those films had a purpose: they were the exposure of the underworld and of the consequences of an unnatural law, Prohibition. They showed things as they were . . . *Little Caesar* was an affirmation of what was right and what was not . . . Mervyn LeRoy produced it with the intention of making the public aware and angry about the crime czars who were getting rich while they suffered with the Depression."*

Robinson's strutting, emphatic performance gave the character a kind of universal status. Eager critics, responding to the actor's large conception, claimed that Robinson gave tragic heightening to his gangster's struggle for power. Like tragic heroes, Rico does seem larger than life and he also seems to be hounded by fate (his death by shooting is inevitable), but his story, finally, is melodrama rather than tragedy. Robinson dresses up the character, but Little Caesar is still a cheap, nervy con man who got exactly what was coming to him.

Robinson spent the rest of his career trying to outlive the success of *Little Caesar*. His ambitious, cocky gangster had the kind of dynamic style that movie audiences wanted to see more of. Robinson played the part so effectively that he was faced with the job of proving that he was not simply playing himself.

Robinson fought Warners for the chance to do other kinds of roles (he did, of course, play a variety of non-gangster parts), but his identification with a thirties-style tough guy nagged him for the rest of his career. As late as 1962, a television columnist complained that Robinson was miscast as the host of a cops-and-robbers special: "Why should an actor who more than any other I can think of is associated with Al Capone type roles be elected to deliver a lecture on crime? No doubt Mr. Robinson is as upright in his private life as any of us, but his public features are etched in the public mind as those of a gangster. He looks far more sinister than the real Al Capone . . . You might as well have Tarzan as the narrator of a documentary on the men's clothing industry."*

Branded as the Boss, the Godfather, the ruler of the roost, Robinson spent most of the thirties playing vigorous authoritarians. He controlled San Francisco during the gold rush in *Barbary Coast* (1935), he was a top fight promoter in *Kid Galahad* (1937), a hard-hitting tabloid editor in *Five Star Final* (1931), a Chinese warlord in *The Hatchet Man* (1932), a colossally successful prospector in *Silver Dollar* (1932), a gambling king in *Smart Money* (1931), a beer baron in *A Slight Case of Murder* (1938). Whatever the enterprise, Robinson was sure to be at the top. Having made his impact as a character who thrusts his way to power in the underworld, the actor continued to play men who are involved in shady deals.

Right after *Little Caesar*, Robinson was especially anxious to

---

*Interview with Gabe Essoe, *Los Angeles Times*, May 25, 1969.

*Jack Iams, *New York Herald Tribune*, March 19, 1962.

THE HATCHET MAN (1932). As Wong Low Get

SILVER DOLLAR (1932). As Yates Martin

prove his versatility. He announced that in his next movie he would portray a deformed balletmaster in the Imperial Russian Ballet. That project, *The Idol*, was never made, but the two-year period after *Little Caesar* was the most spectacular of Robinson's career. In addition to his gamblers and prospectors and yellow journalists, he played a Portuguese fisherman in *Tiger Shark* (1932) and a victimized workingman in *Two Seconds* (1932). In not one of the six films made in 1931 and 1932 was Robinson a conventional gangster. Inevitably, his authority figures and his brash, enterprising characters contained echoes of Rico, but the backgrounds were different, and with the minor exception of the foolish *Hatchet Man*, the films themselves had a freshness and vigor that matched Robinson's own enthusiasm.

The only film in this busy period that seems merely a star vehicle is *Smart Money* (1931), the follow-up to *Little Caesar*, in which Robinson plays a gambler who makes good. The film has exactly the same structure as its predecessor: Robinson is a small-town boy who goes to the big city to earn some dishonest money. This time, the adventurer is a barber turned professional gambler, but Nick Venezelos (Robinson switched from Italian to Greek) has the same pluck and determination as Rico Bandello. At first, retaining his country ways, he's chiseled by big-city slickers and taken for a ride by sharpshooters and dames who are more knowing than he is. But Nick learns. Soon he's head of the biggest gambling casino in town, and dressed nattily in custom-tailored suits, white spats, top hat and cane, he is undisputed cock o' the walk.

Like Little Caesar, Nick has a human weakness (this time it's a passion for blondes) that does him in: he's tricked by a woman he trusted, and his gambling syndicate crumbles as he's sent off to jail. The character's gushing fondness for women softens the edges of his story; *Smart Money* is a lighter and more agreeable portrait than *Little Caesar* of how to make it in underworld Depression America. Robinson's sturdy hero, with his compulsive laugh and his jaunty walk, his resilience even at the end, when, going off to jail, he poses grandly for photographers, is a healthier version of the Little Caesar archetype. The character is a flop with women, but that Nick is persistently beguiled by two-timing blondes adds a kind of raffish charm that's missing from Rico's history.

By and large, Nick is a soft touch for women, and his greenhorn confidence is offset by the unvarying skepticism of his partner (played by James Cagney) who distrusts the entire sex. *Smart Money* contains a

SMART MONEY (1931). With James Cagney

SMART MONEY (1931). With Boris Karloff (at left) and James Cagney (at right)

sly reprise of the famous grapefruit scene in *The Public Enemy:* at breakfast Cagney ominously carves a grapefruit while he scowls at Robinson's latest mistress.

This was the only time that Warners cast their two top tough guys in the same movie. Cagney's role is small and he's subdued, but the two actors with similar staccato deliveries play well together. Robinson is the teacher, Cagney the respectful student who wisely does not try to compete; he hands the older actor their scenes together, and yet he's hardly self-effacing—all the vigor and power are evident, but held in check. In an argument over the woman who turns him in, Robinson throws Cagney to the floor; Cagney hits his head and dies. It's a false note in an otherwise

FIVE STAR FINAL (1931). With Boris Karloff

bright and vivid period piece.

Robinson's managing editor in *Five Star Final* was another smart-talking boss figure, and this time the milieu is even further removed than *Smart Money* from the grim big-city underworld of *Little Caesar*. Departing from the psychotic, woman-hating image of Rico Bandello, Robinson's editor is a dashing figure; his secretary (Aline MacMahon) is crazy about him, and the way Robinson plays him, it's certainly possible to understand her feelings. Robinson acts Randall with great high spirits. A corsage in his vest, his white buck shoes propped up on the desk, his hat pushed back, his cigar dangling from his lips, Robinson never seemed more zestful and youthful. He was really playing a stereotypical notion of a hard-driving, muckraking editor—the contours of the role had already been established by the late twenties, with Hecht

TIGER SHARK (1932). With J. Carrol Naish and Zita Johann

TWO SECONDS (1932). With Vivienne Osborne

and MacArthur's successful *The Front Page*. Shouting on the phone, barking orders to his flunkies, sprucing up for his secretary, Robinson added nothing original to the characterization—he played the editor as a type. But the rapid-fire delivery and the hyped-up manner were appropriate to the story's strong melodramatic flavor. Like Robinson's acting, this film about a yellow journalist who reforms when he sees that the press has the power to destroy innocent lives is blunt, crude, powerful.

Tiger Shark was the first major Robinson triangle movie; here, in the tradition set by *Lady to Love*, Robinson is the older man married to a young woman (Zita Johann) who

TWO SECONDS (1932). The last prayer before execution

falls in love with an eligible young bachelor (Richard Arlen). Playing a simple-minded, excitable Portuguese sea captain, Robinson has to be both avuncular and menacing, a peculiar combination that, in fact, marks many of his characterizations. The character of Mike Mascarena is sweet, gullible, idealistic—a good fellow, in short—but he is a fiend when aroused. He wants to kill his young rival, but at the point of attack, Mike is caught in a rope, flung overboard, and dies.

The role was one of Robinson's favorites: "I adored *Tiger Shark* because I admired Howard Hawks, and I think the reason I admired him is because he let me chew the scenery. As the best tuna fisherman on the West Coast, with one hand already lost to a shark, a curly ebony wig and a flowing mustachio, I had the time of my life."* Here was the kind of bravura "acting" part that Robinson coveted; here was a chance to transform his appearance, to change the timbre and inflection of his voice (Robinson spent weeks with Portuguese fishermen to prepare for the role), to escape emphatically the "curse" of *Little Caesar*. It's a part that uses the actor's unromantic looks—the whole story is predicated on the character's unsuitability for a beautiful woman—but Robinson emerges as the film's most sympathetic character. The Portuguese accent is understated, but Robinson performs in a broad, lush style in the kind of showpiece role that he found harder to get later in the decade.

Two Seconds, his third film with Mervyn LeRoy, presents Robinson in another experimental mood. He's a riveter who has none of the aspirations of the Robinson climbers; he wants a steady job and a nice woman. (The film, in contrast to the gangster cycle, shows what it was like to be honest and poor during the Depression.) Good-natured and passive, plain, unethnic John Allen falls into the clutches of a designing dame (Vivienne Osborne) who takes him for all his modest worth. Guilt-ridden and despondent over his responsibility for the death of his best buddy (Preston Foster), John Allen allows his two-timing wife to dominate him.

He finally catches her with her dance-hall boss and, having been pushed beyond endurance, he shoots her. He's sentenced to the electric chair: the film, in fact, is his review, during the proverbial "two seconds" it takes for him to be electrocuted, of the events leading up to the killing.

Dance halls, beer parlors, tawdry luncheonettes, dingy rooming houses—the film has a strong low-life, working-class atmosphere. Against these grim Depression set-

---

*Robinson, *All My Yesterdays*, p. 126.

BARBARY COAST (1935). With Frank Craven and Miriam Hopkins

tings, Robinson plays a perennial loser and sweet-natured dreamer who is jostled by a relentlessly ironic fate into becoming a murderer. From the early scenes of bantering masculine camaraderie and shy courtship, to the middle section of marital squabbles, depression and withdrawal, to the last great curve from the murder to the impassioned self-justification before the judge, this is a bravura role that Robinson attacks with relish.

The climactic scene, in which Allen defends the murder, explaining that it was an act of manly courage that released him from his dependence on his vicious wife, is a tour de force, one of Robinson's most flamboyant passages. Director Mervyn LeRoy gives the star a dramatic framework for the speech: the character is picked out from the surrounding darkness by a theatrical spotlight. At the climax of his defense, the character explodes in a

BARBARY COAST (1935). With Edward Gargan and Walter Brennan

torrent of tears and rage. It's the crowning touch to a performance that should be much better known than it is.

After this period of high achievement following *Little Caesar*, Robinson's work for the rest of the decade was less original, and in fact, with the exception of *The Whole Town's Talking* (1935), he was never given the sort of challenge he wanted until *Dr. Ehrlich's Magic Bullet* in 1940. Most of Robinson's subsequent thirties work, after the banner year of 1932, had inevitable echoes of his archetypal gangster. Almost inescapably, he was cast as a powerful avaricious operator. His heroes usually flourish in a context that, if not distinctly underworld, is at least tainted with subterfuge and double-dealing. Of his numerous post-*Caesar* boss figures, the kingpins of *Barbary Coast* and *Kid Galahad* are the most persuasive.

Both are tyrants. Both, beneath the inevitable swagger, are sexually disturbed, emotionally disfigured. Typically, too, both characters have a gentlemanly code that underlies the gruff and grimly purposeful exterior, and both, being victims of their own zealous overreaching, are ultimately losers. As always, Robinson turns potential maniacs into humanly understandable characters.

In *Barbary Coast*, Robinson is once again the preternaturally successful man of shady affairs who remains womanless. Unlike Rico Bandello, though, town boss Louis Chamalis wants romance; he even pleads for love from his gambling-hall queen Swan (Miriam Hopkins), but she can offer only friendship as her heart belongs to a poet-prospector named Jim (Joel McCrea). Despite his political power, Chamalis remains an outsider, a misfit. With his foreign name and his decidedly ethnic appearance, he's a social outcast, and clearly no match for the handsome, sensitive poet.

There's often a scene in a Robinson movie when his character cracks, revealing the demons that lurk beneath the authoritative mask. Here, the stripping-down occurs when Chamalis begs Swan to love him. When she refuses, he rages at her as if she were one of his henchmen. In this outburst, the character reveals the depth of his pathetic maladjustment. As is frequently the case with Robinson's strivers, the grasping for power seems to compensate for the inability to give and receive love.

As with Little Caesar, it's the tyrant's strong feelings for a person he cannot control that precipitates his doom. Chamalis is a menace, and the town forms a posse to hunt him down. At the end, hounded, like Little Caesar, into a corner, Chamalis proves to be a gentleman. He lets the lady go off with the poet, and he gives himself up to the people he had ruled so ruthlessly. His final gesture—hat raised cavalierly to the departing lady—has perhaps more charm than Robinson's characterization previously suggested, but the humanity and the irony that the renunciation indicates were in the actor's portrait all along.

Fogbound, rain-soaked, damp and dreary boom town San Francisco (atmospherically rendered in Howard Hawks' direction and the Ben Hecht-Charles MacArthur screenplay) provides an appropriately sinister background for Robinson's twisted mobster. The fight game setting for *Kid Galahad* offers a similarly evocative context for Robinson's disturbed promoter.

In this movie, Robinson's Nick

KID GALAHAD (1937). With Bette Davis

Donati has a problem with his sister (Jane Bryan). When a young fighter (Wayne Morris) whose career he's managing falls for his sister, Robinson bitterly turns against his protégé. Until the last moment, when he has a characteristic change of heart, he threatens to fix the big fight against his man. Nick's reaction is extreme; he's overly protective, having moved his mother and sister to the country in order to shield them from big city corruption. He thinks of women as being either virgins or whores, either pure (and therefore unable to contend with the world) or tough (like his mistress Fluff who can handle herself in a harsh, competitive man's world like the fight game).

Robinson is once again edged out at the end; he's killed in a locker-room shoot-out with a nasty rival manager (Humphrey Bogart).

THE LAST GANGSTER (1937). With Lionel Stander.

As in *Barbary Coast*, his removal clears the way for romance. With the sour, disapproving Robinson character out of the way, the young lovers are freed. But Robinson did not think of Nick as one of his anti-romantic roles: "It has softer moments, the romantic element is strongly stressed ... there is an odd sort of romance between Nick and Fluff but it is warm and sincere, nevertheless."* It's true that he and Fluff (Bette Davis) have a mature understanding, but their real passion is directed elsewhere—Robinson's, toward protecting his sister's virginity, Davis', toward the unattainable Kid Galahad.

Under Michael Curtiz' direction, Robinson's performance as the oddly obsessed manager is tart, but for once he doesn't quite dominate a film. As the kindhearted mistress who falls for the Kid, and who smothers her feelings in honor of young love, Bette Davis plays with a warmth that claims the movie as hers. *Kid Galahad* was designed as a Robinson movie, but it turns out instead to be an uncharacteristic Davis film.

As the decade advanced, and the gangster cycle that began with *Little Caesar* and *The Public Enemy* ran quickly through its heyday, Robinson moved along with the changing fashions. Beginning with *Little Giant* in 1933, he played in a series of comic variations on the gangster genre, and together with Cagney he moved in mid-decade to the other side of the law. By 1937 the original gangster formula had been so exhausted that Robinson made a tired movie at MGM (a studio singularly ill-equipped for the kind of hard-edged crime story that Warners turned out) called, significantly, *The Last Gangster*.

In comedies like *Little Giant, The Whole Town's Talking* (1935) and *A Slight Case of Murder* (1938), Robinson was burlesquing himself. Movie tastes had changed, and the gangster-as-hero that audiences had taken seriously in the early thirties became, as early as 1935, a figure of fun rather than menace. John Ford's splendid comedy, *The Whole Town's Talking*, made sport of the tough gangster image that Robinson had popularized. In this crime comedy, Little Caesar plays both himself and his look-alike, a steady, mousy clerk who's mistaken for the gangster by an overzealous citizen. Robinson's vigorous, burly boss, his voice lowered ominously, is standard stuff by this time, but his clerk, who dominates the film, was a revelation. Quiet, sweet-natured and winsome, a fussy bachelor and a hard worker, Arthur Ferguson Jones is one of Robinson's most refreshing characterizations. Blessed with one

---

*Interview with Regina Crewe, *New York American*, May 23, 1937.

THE WHOLE TOWN'S TALKING (1935). As Arthur Ferguson Jones and "Killer" Mannion

of the trickiest roles of his career, Robinson never overdoes it; even as he plays Jones impersonating "Killer" Mannion, Robinson's touch remains light. For once, Robinson does not stress the fact that he's playing a virtuoso role, and his double meek clerk-nasty criminal characterization is the deftest comedy performance of his career.

Robinson's comic gangster in *A Slight Case of Murder* —a Damon Runyon beer baron whose way of life collapses with the repeal of Prohibition—is less successful. With no choice but to turn honest, he retreats to his country house to begin his assault on straight society.

With four fresh corpses deposited in his living room, it is no wonder the beer baron never makes it as a respectable bourgeois.

With its elaborate plot contrivances and its hectic pace, the film, unlike the more delicate Ford film, is out-and-out farce. It's interesting for the changes in sensibility it suggests, but it's strained, agitated comedy. Robinson offers a broad parody of Little Caesar—the rhetorical delivery and the assertive hand gestures are more pronounced than ever—but he's no farceur. Ruth Donnelly as his wife gives the sharpest performance. She plays a tough dame, every bit her husband's equal, who tries to ease into her new role of society matron by affecting an upper-crust accent. Her rapid alternation between uppity matron and lowdown dame, and her occasional confusion of roles, provide incisive social comment. By comparison, Robinson's work seems monotonous.

Connected to these comic gangsters was the series of parts in which Robinson was cast as a vulgarian. (*Little Caesar* seemed to have disqualified him from respectability.) In several minor formula pictures in 1933 and 1934 (*Dark Hazard*, *I Loved a Woman*, and *Little Giant*), Robinson is cast as a tycoon whose questionable business interests and whose low-life friends disbar him from the country-club set. In these roles, Robinson played men who fatally lacked class.

Robinson is another gambler in *Dark Hazard* (dog races this time); a meat packer who sells tainted beef in *I Loved a Woman;* a beer baron in *Little Giant*. Later in the decade, in *Thunder in the City* in 1937, his "vulgarity" is transported to England, where he serves as an archetypically brash American salesman. He's a go-getter, a show-off, whose cockiness is sharply contrasted to British reserve. In all of these minor films, Robinson is used as a shifty American entrepreneur, aggressive and adamant, but also put upon: he's mocked for his coarse manners, rejected for his looks, double-crossed by business associates. Women spurn him, give him the runaround, goad him. In *Little Giant*, society makes fun of him—until they discover he's a millionaire. In *I Loved a Woman*, a snobbish opera singer thinks he isn't good enough for her, until the end, when he finally proves himself to her satisfaction. In *Dark Hazard*, his puritanical small-town wife objects to his gambling. She leaves him for a more refined and tamable man, and Robinson returns to his dog races.

Little Giant is the best of these modest pictures. Robinson here played the first of his comic variations on gangster stereotypes; as in *A Slight Case of Murder* four years

A SLIGHT CASE OF MURDER (1938). With Paul Harvey, Ruth Donnelly, and Jane Bryan

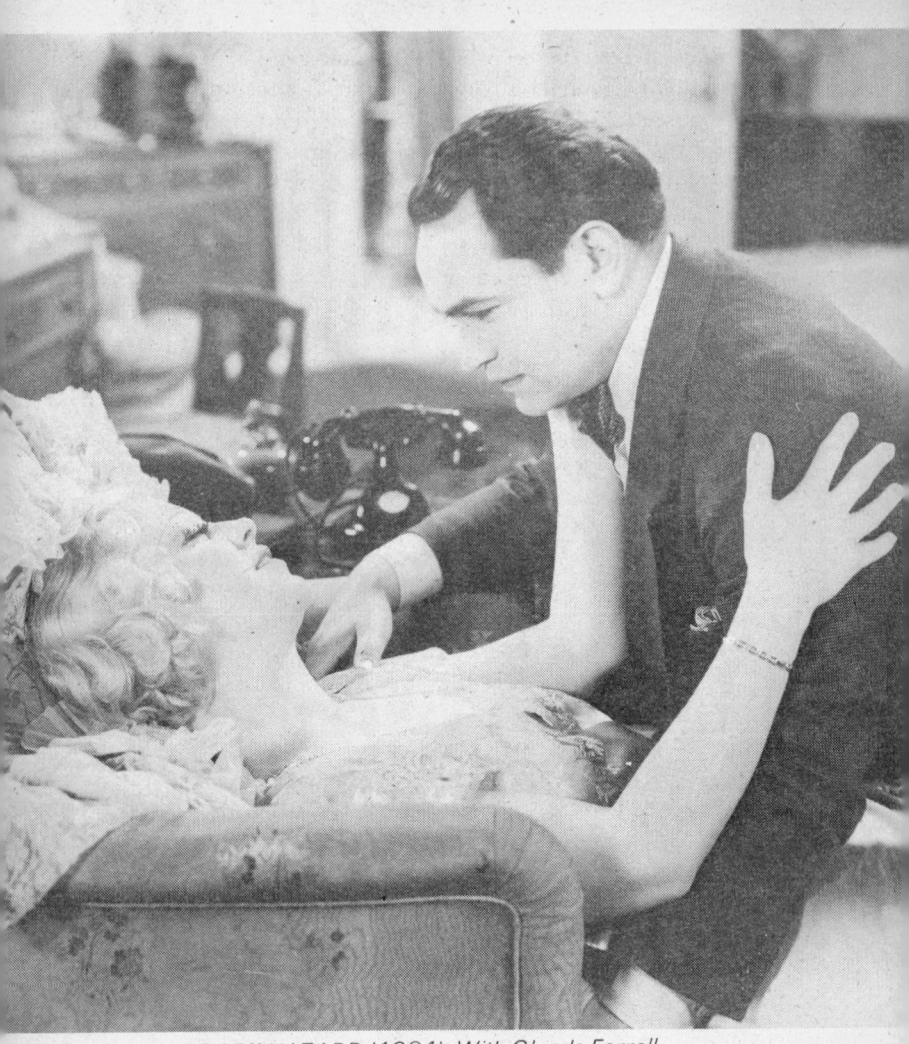
DARK HAZARD (1934). With Glenda Farrell

later, he plays a beer baron who tries to go straight. Though his New York street manner disqualifies him from a swank California country club, in the end he gets the better of some fake aristocrats, and is welcomed by the real McCoy. Quick-witted and resourceful, the little giant proves that he's "acceptable" after all.

Having set the style, early in the decade, for portraying movie gangsters, Robinson had to work hard to earn the right to play respectable characters. Following his success as Little Caesar, Robinson spent time cleaning up his image; playing comic and ultimately lovable con men was one way of doing it. It was a long struggle, and not until 1940, when Warners let him play Dr. Ehrlich, did the actor get a role in an entirely non-crime film.

The last gasp of Robinson's effort to clear his name occurs in *Blackmail* (1939). His character has triumphed over a spotty past by becoming a prosperous businessman. Sentenced to a chain gang for a crime he didn't commit, he escaped and has done penance by living a model middle-class life: he's an exemplary husband and father. (This was one of the few times Robinson was seen on film as a family man.) The thug who committed the crime Robinson was accused of returns to blackmail him; tricked by the con artist, Robinson is sent off again to the chain gang, where he is brutally treated. In the end, after much suffering, after being scapegoat and victim, he is reinstated in the community.

His character here isn't entitled to middle-class contentment until he's proven himself through trial by fire. It's as if the character, like Robinson himself, must exorcise the shadow of the criminal that hangs over him. Bosley Crowther's comment in *The New York Times* was typical of the critics who thought Robinson was misplacing his energies in seeking respectability: "What a sad thing to see this distinguished inhabitant of the Rogues' Gallery, this Napoleon of crime, this indomitably amoral spirit who belongs with the Borgias, trying to go straight."

Robinson also polished his image in switching to the other side of the law. His role in *Bullets or Ballots* (1936) suggests the shift in moviegoers' tastes. By 1936, it was no longer potent box office to romanticize criminals; the glamour and the titillation of crook-as-hero had diminished, and movies began instead to make heroes of cops and detectives. No longer confined to the sidelines, and portrayed as either dim-witted or crazed (the cop in *Little Caesar* is the most repellent character in the film), the police became the center of attention in crime films; for the first time,

THUNDER IN THE CITY (1937). With Nigel Bruce and Ralph Richardson

I LOVED A WOMAN (1933). With Kay Francis

LITTLE GIANT (1933). With Mary Astor

BLACKMAIL (1939). With Arthur Hohl (at left)

they were allowed full-scale personalities. And with Robinson and Cagney playing them, G-men were assured of being portrayed with vitality.

In *Bullets or Ballots*, Robinson and his superior officer are the sharpest guys in town. It's the members of the gang who are now the pale stereotypes. Robinson's role is one of those double parts he was always so fond of: he plays a police officer who pretends to defect from the force by joining a gang. Robinson as make-believe gangster was of course convincing; he carried with him the daredevil brashness that had served Little Caesar so well. Except for a skeptical Humphrey Bogart, Robinson's mas-

THE AMAZING DR. CLITTERHOUSE (1938). With Maxie Rosenbloom, Claire Trevor, and Humphrey Bogart

querade fools the gang. Robinson liked the challenge of the role playing: "It was a hard part—I had to play it differently from those gangsters roles, play it down, make it quieter . . . Even so, in that scene where I had to convince the audience as well as the gang that I was turning racketeer, I could see a trace of Little Caesar again."*

*Interview in the *New York Sun*, June 16, 1936.

The character proves he's a hero by dying for the cause of gangbusting. His greatest "acting" is to go through with the final charade, in which he delivers the top brass to the police, while suffering from a bullet wound. Robinson's career is littered with death scenes, but his expiration here is one of his grandest.

Even as fake mobster, Robinson was still implicated in the gang milieu. In *Bullets or Ballots* he re-

THE MAN WITH TWO FACES (1934). As Damon Wells (in disguise)

mains uncorrupted by the gang, but two years later, in *The Amazing Dr. Clitterhouse,* his double-dealing character capitulates to the lure of crime. Robinson is a society doctor (it was his most socially elevated character to date) who observes criminals at work. Detached at first, he becomes more and more intrigued by the challenge and excitement of the criminal's life. His spirit of scientific inquiry dwindles, and Clitterhouse ends up deeply involved in a life of crime: ultimately, he's head of a gang of jewel thieves, and a murderer.

Robinson was compared unfavorably to Cedric Hardwicke, who originated the role of Clitterhouse on Broadway. A crusty Englishman, Sir Cedric had the society manner that the part required; with Robinson, the drawing room poise seemed external. In *The New York Times* (July 21, 1938), Frank Nugent complained, "It is easier to think of Robinson as a criminal masquerading as a physician than as a medico fronting as a gang lord . . . he never quite succeeds in shaking the role free from the shadowy public enemies, numbers one to ten, which have been the larger part of his past."

I AM THE LAW (1938). With John Beal and Barbara O'Neil

CONFESSIONS OF A NAZI SPY (1939). As Federal agent Ed Renard

In addition to the characters in *Bullets or Ballots* and *The Amazing Dr. Clitterhouse* who wandered disguised through crime settings, Robinson enacted another charade in the earlier film, *The Man With Two Faces* (1934). This time, as in *Bullets or Ballots*, he traps a criminal for a good cause. He's a vain actor who disguises himself with wig, whiskers, false eyebrows, putty nose, and French accent in order to wreak revenge on his sister's fiendish tormentor.

Robinson always liked dressing up for his characters, disguising his face and voice, experimenting with different styles and movement; he eagerly sought these tricky, Pirandellian roles in films like *Man With Two Faces* and *The Amazing Dr. Clitterhouse*, and he sometimes complained that he didn't get enough of these characters who "act."

After playing a double-dealing G-man in *Bullets or Ballots*, Robinson graduated to straight law enforcement roles in *I Am the Law* (1938) and *Confessions of a Nazi Spy* (1939). In the former, he's a law professor turned racket buster. Robinson approaches his job with the same enthusiasm he had dem-

CONFESSIONS OF A NAZI SPY (1939). With Paul Lukas

onstrated for playing public enemies—he's earnest and unshakable—but audiences were still skeptical. In the *New York Herald Tribune* (August 26, 1938), Howard Barnes commented: "It seems evident that Robinson is determined to make filmgoers forget that he was once the archetype of the gangster . . . It is my hunch, though, that he is still not at home in heroic roles . . . he is at his best when he is mussing up three thugs to show his staff how yellow they really are . . . It's still hard for me to keep in mind that he is a cleaner-upper."

In *Confessions of a Nazi Spy*, as a tireless FBI investigator bent on ridding the country of Nazi agitators, Robinson had a distinctly supporting role which he played with a stern propriety that had not figured in his work before this. The "acting" parts went to the Nazis, who are portrayed as a group of maniacs. In *The New York Times* (April 29, 1939), Frank Nugent questioned the film's accuracy: "Membership in the National Socialist Party cannot be restricted entirely to the rat-faced, the brute-browed, the sinister. We don't believe Nazi propaganda Ministers let their mouths twitch evilly whenever they mention our Constitution or Bill of Rights."

Robinson's restraint counteracts the operatics of George Sanders and Paul Lukas, as the principal crackpot Nazis. Robinson is the steadfast law enforcer, the sober representative of the American Way. His most understated work of the decade, his acting here was a premonition of a subtler, mellower style that distinguished much of his work in the forties and fifties.

ROBINSON IN THE FORTIES: EHRLICH TO ROCCO

Along with small parts in omnibus movies and leading roles in minor formula pictures, Robinson in the forties was given the toughest challenges of his career. As the dedicated and pioneering *Dr. Ehrlich* (1940); as the demonic Wolf Larsen in *The Sea Wolf* (1941); as the doggedly determined claims investigator in *Double Indemnity* (1944); as the wistful farmer in *Our Vines Have Tender Grapes* (1945); as the meek man turned criminal in *Woman in the Window* (1945) and *Scarlet Street* (1946); as the self-deceived businessman in *All My Sons* (1948); as the sadistic crook trying for a comeback in *Key Largo* (1948); and as the vitriolic Sicilian patriarch in *House of Strangers* (1949), Robinson flourished, contributing a series of full-bodied characterizations in which he was working at top capacity. Though, of course, there were echoes of the classic thirties Robinson, these performances were largely free from stereotype.

Robinson didn't magically transform his persona for each new role—his signature was apparent in everything he did—but he was not simply transposing a ready-made, studio-created personality from film to film either. At his slackest, when he was bored by the material, when his role called for little more than a repeat performance, he was content to do his vaudevillean routine. But in his strongest forties roles, he rediscovered himself for each assignment, and the kind of versatility that he had been applauded for on the stage in the twenties was pointedly visible in films.

These high Robinson performances were delivered in a variety of genres, from biography to domestic drama to psychological melodrama to *film noir* to a return, in *Key Largo*, to the classic gangster mold. Even here, though, the range of types was not exceptionally varied; there were no musicals, for instance, no historical romances, no romantic comedies, no Westerns. But the films at least provided variations on the urban crime background that was the usual territory for the Robinson persona; the actor connected to crime in new ways, most often from the outside, as an unwilling participant or as an investigator. More pronounced in the actor's forties criminals was their deviate nature; *The Sea Wolf* and the Fritz Lang melodramas *(Woman in the Window* and *Scarlet Street),* for instance, offer the kind of psychological probing that was largely missing

DR. EHRLICH'S MAGIC BULLET (1940). As Dr. Paul Ehrlich

THE SEA WOLF (1941). As Wolf Larsen

A DISPATCH FROM REUTERS (1940). With Gene Lockhart (seated at right)

from the thirties films. At his most fevered pitch, Robinson played different kinds of madmen; he was often a man possessed—by so mundane a preoccupation as a job in *Double Indemnity,* by a barn in *Our Vines Have Tender Grapes,* by money in *All My Sons,* by power in *The Sea Wolf* and *Key Largo,* and at the most exalted level, by an Idea in *Dr. Ehrlich's Magic Bullet.*

The driven Robinson hero dominates these major performances. Robinson is almost always the alienated figure ravaged by powerful subterranean forces. Whether victim, as in the Lang films, or victimizer, as in *The Sea Wolf* and *Key Largo,* Robinson's characters are often self-tortured. Protected by his craggy looks from leading-man blandness, Robinson played men who were isolated by the force of their obsessions. Only in his two

BROTHER ORCHID (1940). With Ann Sothern

biographical films, *Dr. Ehrlich's Magic Bullet* and *A Dispatch from Reuters* (1940), did Robinson play largely conventional heroes. The rest of the time he was often too tormented to relate in a normal way to the world around him; only in the highly atypical *Our Vines Have Tender Grapes* does he play a character who fits snugly into the pattern of the community.

The embattled loner, usually pursuing without the support of family or friends the goals that consume him, Robinson is certainly no romantic hero, and he hardly qualifies as a hip, charismatic antihero either. He is the least sentimental of the great movie actors. At his most forceful, in *The Sea Wolf, Double Indemnity,* and *Key Largo,* he's terrifying in his aggressiveness, and yet he almost always makes us care for his misfits. His authoritarian characters are always vulnerable, and in showing us what's beneath the insinuating masks, Robinson humanizes his dictators. He transforms his demons of power and revenge into characters that are at least comprehensible, if not exactly likable. Given a villainous part, Robinson can be frightening, but at his best he isn't simply in the business of marketing Grand Guignol histrionics: his bad guys have psychological histories that connect them to the world at large.

Robinson fought his studio for the part of Dr. Paul Ehrlich, the discoverer of Salvarsan, the remedy for syphilis, and he felt the results established his credentials as a serious, flexible actor. Like other Warners contract players, Robinson objected to type-casting and to indifferent assignments, and he regarded Dr. Ehrlich as the part that at last gave him a chance at "class." During the thirties, he had been rankling, too, over the fact that Warners had graduated Paul Muni, another alumnus of the gangster film, to prestige roles in *The Story of Louis Pasteur* and *The Life of Emile Zola*. Robinson believed that his arch-rival Muni had been elevated to dignified star status—had been allowed to "act"—while he had been confined to repetitive genre items. The truth, of course, was that Muni began to take himself too seriously, while Robinson, never allowed to go highbrow, remained more versatile and usable.

Dr. Ehrlich was Robinson's favorite part; to get it, he even agreed to do yet another comic take-off on his hoodlum persona. In order to play the distinguished doctor, he consented to be *Brother Orchid* (1940), a con man who ends up tending flowers in a monastery.

Believing himself on home ground at last, using the role as conclusive proof that Little Caesar had only been an acting stunt after all, Robinson erased all the mannerisms that had become standard currency for his crime world characters. The voice is studiously subdued, the usually staccato delivery muted and slowed down to a hum. Robinson moves through the film in hushed tones that suggest a reverence for the character. At odd, fleeting moments, with a finger too sharply crooked at an adversary, or a syllable too harshly spoken, a gesture too sporty or aggressive, we catch glimpses of the patented Robinson. But for most of the film he plays with a different kind of authority from that of the mobster. A jubilant Robinson told reporters at the time: "You can't imagine the pleasure I got out of doing that part. So far, most of the rats, detectives, prosecutors and editors I've played were two-dimensional characters, and it was up to me to round them out, give them flesh and blood, and the qualities of human beings. But Ehrlich is a different matter altogether. The character is there—and a great character it is—all an actor has to do is to play it honestly and simply."*

In this film, Robinson is a solitary thinker, inspired by humanitarian motives rather than by the struggle for power, Ehrlich is nonetheless linked to earlier Robinson heroes in his single-mindedness, his ability to elicit devotion from his followers, and his fearless rule breaking. Challenged on all sides by narrow bureaucrats, ill-treated by skeptical colleagues, Ehrlich stubbornly pursues his research into a disease regarded with shocked abhorrence in his day.

Faced with what he considered at the time to be his most spacious role, Robinson proceeds with restraint, and his performance is excellent; the actor left no doubt that he could transcend stereotype. But finally *Dr. Ehrlich's Magic Bullet,* directed by William Dieterle, is a dreadfully boring movie, and Robinson as a world-renowned scientist is much less colorful than in his series of vigorous portraits of undignified crooks. Playing what is, after all, a conventional movie biography hero, Robinson is much less of an individual than he ever was before.

Like the actor, the filmmakers too were conscious of working on a distinguished property, and the movie pays more attention to test tubes, microscopes, diagrams, and scientific explanations than to personal drama. Determined to be uplifting and educational in dealing with a touchy—in fact taboo—subject, the film plays down the usual conflicts and setbacks of biographical drama in favor of documentary-like authenticity. Everyone, including Ruth Gordon as Ehrlich's sweetly supportive, tea-serving wife, is on his best upper-crust behavior. Critics fell for

*Interview with the *New York Post*, February 16, 1940.

DR. EHRLICH'S MAGIC BULLET (1940). Dr. Ehrlich in his laboratory

DR. EHRLICH'S MAGIC BULLET (1940). The doctor and his colleagues

the high-toned treatment, calling the film "a veritable milestone in the history of the movies" (*Life*, March 4, 1940), a film that "holds high promise for the future of the screen" (Howard Barnes, the *New York Herald Tribune*, February 24, 1940). But Otis Ferguson had the last and truest word when he wrote, "A test tube is a test tube and a picture is a picture."

Intelligent and earnest as he is in the role, Robinson as Ehrlich is really no fun at all: he's a big actor cramped in what is basically a narrow, monochromatic part. Fortunately, only once again in his restless search for parts in which to hide himself did he hit upon a dullard. His Norwegian farmer in *Our Vines Have Tender Grapes* is another blatantly non-Robinson part, and this time, he doesn't quite manage the transformation.

The farmer Martinius Jacobson is probably his most uncharacteristic role, and the MGM film in which the character appears is a direct contrast to the tough Warners movies indelibly associated with Robinson. It is as representative of *its* studio as *Little Caesar*, *Bullets or Ballots* or *Kid Galahad* is of Warners-First National.

Presented as a series of vignettes set in an immigrant farming community in Wisconsin, the film is quintessential MGM family fare —relentlessly wholesome and inspirational. Cast extravagantly against type, Robinson plays a quiet family man rather than his customary driven loner. In this one he doesn't want to take over the North Side or to be absolute master of his own ship or even to cure syphilis: he only wants a new barn. He enjoys the quiet life of a farmer; evenings are spent at home around the fireside, and it's church on Sundays.

Robinson is the wise and kindly father who explains loneliness, patience, tolerance, and death to his wide-eyed daughter (Margaret O'Brien). At the end, after the church service, walking down a country path shaded by blossoming trees, Robinson says to his daughter that they've both been going through a period of growth.

The actor uses his subdued Dr. Ehrlich approach again; his principal assumption in playing against type is that less is more. His work here is remarkably casual and low-key; Robinson again whispers much of his dialogue. This time, though, the quiet, dignified manner is less effective. He often looks uncomfortable in this papier-mâché MGM countryside, and he and Agnes Moorehead are too old to be O'Brien's parents, and too quirky and individual, despite their charade, to fit into the homogenized community the film sets up. There are moments when Robinson gets hold of the character,

OUR VINES HAVE TENDER GRAPES (1945). With Margaret O'Brien and Agnes Moorehead

tearfully responding to his daughter's Sunday School recitation, for instance, or cuddling O'Brien as if Little Caesar had never existed. But there are also times when, with a snarl or a mean look, Robinson subverts the goody-goody atmosphere, slyly sneaking in his own comment on the worth of the material. There are two especially revealing scenes, one in which Martinius snaps at his daughter, ordering her to go to bed, and another in which, gun in hand, he goes to shoot cattle who are trapped in a burning barn. In these encounters, the actor responds to his role with an enthusiasm that the material has not encouraged. He can't conceal the glee in his voice or the swagger in his stride when he's given the chance to growl at his daughter or to carry a gun. In injecting sarcastic flourishes and unfriendly looks where they don't belong, it's as if Robinson wants to complicate and darken his role.

Despite fleeting glimpses of the

OUR VINES HAVE TENDER GRAPES (1945). With Margaret O'Brien and Jackie ("Butch") Jenkins

THE SEA WOLF (1941). With Ida Lupino

actor's menacing presence, despite our knowledge of his past performances, Robinson almost makes it; that he works so modestly, handing the film over to whom it belongs —the sensitive child star Margaret O'Brien—is itself something of an achievement. With its MGM-like passage of the seasons, its Hollywood-rustic wholesomeness, its accumulation of country calamities, and its weepy lesson-pointing, *Our Vines Have Tender Grapes* will always be a curiosity in the Robinson canon, an odd and not-quite-convincing departure from the official record.

If in the forties Robinson finally got the chance to explore radical changes from his Little Caesar image, he was also given roles that offered operatic variations on his snarling hood. Dryly understated in unusual roles in *Dr. Ehrlich's Magic Bullet* and *Our Vines Have Tender Grapes,* Robinson was grandiose in

THE SEA WOLF (1941). With John Garfield

his two showcase pieces, *The Sea Wolf* and *Key Largo*. Here the threatening, psychotic figure of the Robinson gangster was given spectacular showcasing: as the tyrannical ship's captain in the Jack London story, and as the mobster hell-bent on a comeback in *Key Largo*, the twisted, power-mad Robinson persona attained its apotheosis. These self-delightedly theatrical performances were two of the actor's grandest statements.

Cruelly dominating his ship in *The Sea Wolf* and establishing rule over an isolated ramshackle hotel in *Key Largo*, Robinson plays obsessed men. Both these unbending tyrants are accorded star entrances; other characters talk about them, and we see the fear they've created before they even appear. Robinson's first scene in *Key Largo* is probably one of the most famous entrances in movies: we discover the character in a cold bath, cigar hanging truculently from his swollen lips, his torso, sagging and pendulous, drenched with sweat. It's a ghastly moment; director John Huston said he wanted to show the naked animal underneath the dressed-up gangster.

In the thirties, Robinson's bad guys were natural products of the Prohibition city. Robinson invested his earlier hoods with psychotic nuances—he supplied complexity where screenplays called mostly for conventional and unexamined villainy—but the characters' deviate psychology was never the real concern of the films. In these two forties variations on the Robinson madman-tyrant, the characters' palpitant abnormality is precisely the films' main focus.

Both films as well have an intellectual self-consciousness that did not detain the coarser, blunter thirties movies. *The Sea Wolf* and *Key Largo*, unlike *Little Caesar* or *Smart Money* or *A Slight Case of Murder*, are ablaze with Higher Intentions; the literary flourishes are a residue from the Jack London and Maxwell Anderson originals, London and Anderson being more self-important writers than W.R. Burnett. The characters, then, are placed within a loftier framework than the one provided by the classic crime movies, but the pretentious showcasing hardly impedes Robinson.

Directed by Michael Curtiz, the actor turns Wolf Larsen into one of American movies' ultimate sadists. Friendless, suspicious, a hulking, brutish grotesque, Robinson's captain runs his ship as if it were a floating insane asylum. He delights in humiliating the ship's doctor, who asks to be treated with respect; he gleefully hands the ship's stoolie to the men, to do with him what they will. When three new passengers come aboard, he quickly finds a way of taunting each of them—he takes

THE SEA WOLF (1941). With Ida Lupino and Gene Lockhart

particular pleasure in humiliating the woman (Ida Lupino) for being an escaped convict. Proud of his place, he makes the whole ship dance to his own mad music. He is a loser who feeds his own shaky ego by surrounding himself with human wrecks, hopeless bums and crooks and alcoholics. A failure in the outside world, Larson has created his own death ship in which he can be uncontested master of a carefully chosen crew.

Typically, Robinson is not content to play the sea wolf as a grotesque cut off altogether from human society; he makes him a cripple rather than a fiend, a man in the grip of some powerful, undefined force that compels him to act in ways that he doesn't always want to. Wolf Larsen has a primal fear of his brother, and he has rigged his ship with cannons so as to withstand an attack from him. Making the feared brother seem like the Furies in pursuit, Robinson turns Larsen into a figure riddled with guilt.

It's a vibrantly physical performance, Robinson fiercely rubbing his aching skull, stomping magisterially on the deck and below quarters, putting on a brave front when, temporarily blinded, he pretends to see. Robinson gives the character height and dignity; he makes the sea wolf the kind of tragic figure that some critics claimed he made of Little Caesar. Though the script has no- where the size of *Moby Dick*, Robinson almost manages to give Larsen the stature of Melville's driven Captain Ahab. What gives the performance its particular tension is the possibility Robinson suggests that Larsen might have been decent and normal. Underneath the diseased mind, there are flashes of the brilliant and cultivated gentleman that might have been. The ambivalence is especially evident in the film's most famous scene, in which a temporarily sightless Robinson appeals to the mercy of one of his prisoners, a writer (Alexander Knox) who is interested in his captor as a case study. Here, in asking for a kind of compassion that he could not himself give, Robinson suggests a flickering humanity, and, like the writer, for a moment we too are beguiled by his apparent reformation. But he quickly reverts to his malevolent self and drags the writer down with him on his sinking ship.

Robinson's character is a self-created tyrant who makes of his ship an image of the world as he sees it. He's a self-aware madman who reads Freud and Jung and who wants to pattern himself on the great literary psychopaths. Robinson vividly conveys the character's crude yet genuine intellect, his strong yearning for self-knowledge. And yet he conveys as well the character's underlying helplessness. Wanting desperately to control his fate, his captain is propelled by forces beyond his power to contain. Naked and grim in its relentless exploration of a doomed soul, Robinson's sea wolf is one of the great psychotics in American films.

John Huston's *Key Largo* is another ode to the vigorous Robinson madman. Here Robinson is once again the kingpin hood surrounded by the inevitable tart and a rogues' gallery of henchmen. The character types are familiar, but the setting is exotic. The gangsters are not enclosed in the big city, but in an isolated, decrepit hotel on one of the southernmost Florida keys. Just returned from Europe and enforced retirement, Robinson and his boys are aiming for a comeback.

Released in 1948, long after the heyday of the gangster movie, *Key Largo* treats its hoods as remnants from an earlier era. They're clearly out of their time, relics of an old order. Like the cowboys in transition Westerns, they've outlived their day. Robinson and his cronies seem to be doing a vaudeville turn in order to remind audiences of the way criminals used to act.

KEY LARGO (1948). With Claire Trevor

KEY LARGO (1948). As Johnny Rocco

Key Largo is also unlike the classic gangster films in insisting on an idea: Robinson and his associates are forced to shoulder a heavy symbolic burden. They are the incarnation of cosmic evil, and when they're eliminated, one by one, the world is cleansed. In the last scene, Lauren Bacall opens a window of the dark hotel, and the room is flooded with holy, purifying light. With Robinson and his cronies bumped off, the moral order has been restored. The material has over it the heavy hand of Maxwell Anderson, and his aggressive philosophizing, largely retained in the Richard Brooks-John Huston screenplay, turns a potentially nifty crime thriller into a bloated tract.

Humphrey Bogart is a former war hero who's forced by the threat of Robinson's gang to abandon his isolationism. When he finally shoots Robinson, Bogart reclaims his heroism. Cast in uncharacteristic roles as the reluctant knight and the modest maiden, Bogey and Bacall are in low gear in this one. They remain subservient to Anderson's noisy "idea"; Robinson, however, easily transcends the script's scheme and turns a symbol into a full-bodied character.

Chomping on a big cigar, gun often in hand, Robinson terrorizes Bogart, Bacall and Lionel Barrymore (as Bacall's morally fastidious father-in-law), holds ruthless sway over his men, and taunts former mistress Claire Trevor, who's been summoned in order to complete his comeback masquerade.

In a famous scene (it won Trevor an Oscar), Robinson makes his floozy sing for a drink. When she's finished her cracked, pathetic rendition of "Moanin' Low," Robinson, with calculated glee, forbids her the drink, pouring it out in front of her. Since Johnny Rocco is something like a final flourish of the classic Robinson hood ("the last of the red-hot gangsters," Bosley Crowther called him), it's fitting that the woman-hating that had always been a part of Robinson's gangster image is emphasized here. Johnny Rocco is cruel to everyone, but he is especially venomous to his moll, rewarding her loyalty with mountainous contempt. Robinson the anti-romantic is evident in another grisly encounter in which he plants a wet, sloppy kiss on a wriggling Lauren Bacall. Robinson behaves as if he were delivering the kiss of death.

It's a broad, fulsome performance, with the actor savoring the possibilities as a reminder, perhaps, of the glory days at First National. The role emphasizes all that's unromantic and menacing in the actor's iconography, all the characteristics that disqualified him right from the start as leading man material. A criminal psychopath and a sexual grotesque, Johnny Rocco is the epitome of "the vulgarity, corruption, and egoism of a criminal man."*

In the storm scene, Rocco has the uncontrollable shakes. As in *The Sea Wolf*, Robinson uses broad physical acting to reveal what's going on inside his character. But this time, Robinson does not humanize his villain; Johnny Rocco is the closest role in the canon to the delineation of pure evil. Performing full speed ahead, Robinson seemed to know that this was the last chance he'd have to play a big-time gangster in a major film. His electric presence subverts Maxwell Anderson's symbolic intentions, and *Key Largo* emerges more a gothic curiosity than a somber message drama.

In addition to roles in which he was cast flamboyantly against type and roles in which he played on his image in the grand manner, Robinson had several strong parts in the forties in which his usual film persona was called into action from odd and intriguing tangents. In *Woman in the Window*, *Scarlet Street*, and *All My Sons*, Robinson is once again a criminal, but the circumstances surrounding his crimes are quite different from those of the Prohibition gang. In these films, the Robinson characters edge into crime against their will; they are all victims of circumstance, moral weaklings, decidedly unheroic criminals who, in moments of panic, act contrary to their usual selves. Their crimes are the gestures of trapped, pathetic little men rather than the grandiose statements of a Rico Bandello, a Wolf Larsen, or a Johnny Rocco. In some of his most famous parts, Robinson played characters with extraordinary personalities, larger-than-life heroes and swaggerers who challenge fate. In these middle-period films, Robinson plays characters in sharp contrast with those who had shaped his image, and these variations on the criminal mentality were more forceful proof of his versatility than his work in *Dr. Ehrlich's Magic Bullet* and *Our Vines Have Tender Grapes*.

The two Fritz Lang melodramas, *Woman in the Window* and *Scarlet Street*, are quintessential *films noirs*, in which murder is linked to repressed sexuality, and in which the city's darkened streets reflect the characters' tortured minds. In both films, the beleaguered Robinson character is pushed against his will into committing a murder. In *Woman in the Window*, Robinson is an urbane psychology professor. A summer bachelor (wife and daughter have been sent to the shore), the professor enjoys leisurely, sedate evenings at his club. Robinson is wonderfully dry in the film's low-key opening; perhaps nowhere else does he dispel so

*Bosley Crowther, *The New York Times*, July 17, 1948.

WOMAN IN THE WINDOW (1944). With Joan Bennett

WOMAN IN THE WINDOW (1944). With Joan Bennett

completely his earlier image as a commoner and vulgarian. Engaging in genteel conversation, enjoying after-dinner coffee in the club's ornate lounge, Robinson is the very model of a cultivated gentleman. The lordly impression is crucial to what follows as the professor's slip into crime is measured against the rarefied and enclosed world in which we first see him.

Admiring a portrait in the window of an art gallery, Professor Wanley is delighted when the subject herself (Joan Bennett) appears to look on with him. Lazily (it's summer, his wife is away, his customary reserve is loosened), he goes with her for a drink, and then permits himself the further luxury of another drink at the woman's apartment. During his visit, a man enters and attacks the professor in a jealous rage. In self-defense, the professor stabs his assailant with a pair of scissors. Instead of reporting the crime, Robinson and the woman decide, fatally, to cover it up. Faced with disposing of the body and concealing a murder, the usually unflustered professor becomes a criminal conspirator.

SCARLET STREET (1946). With Joan Bennett

SCARLET STREET (1946). Christopher Cross, on the skids

The fates are against him. Since the man he killed was a tycoon, the police investigate the case tirelessly. As further aggravation, Professor Wanley's colleagues develop a keen interest in trying to second-guess the killer. All the while, as the net tightens around him, the professor must maintain his usual blandness. The tycoon's bodyguard turns up to harass the conspirators, and Wanley, envisioning an endless sequence of blackmail and self-compromise, takes poison—at which point he is awakened by the steward at his club. He had dozed off over a book, and had imagined the entire scenario.

As the dreamer enmeshed in a catastrophe of his own devising, Robinson is controlled and sly. In much more satisfying ways than the showier roles as Dr. Ehrlich and Farmer Jacobson, Robinson's analytical, untested professor established his ability to transcend the hard-boiled image that plagued him throughout the thirties. His dignified professor is far from being a comedy-of-manners caricature; he never turns the character into a buffoon, and yet he convinces us that this deeply conventional man would cover up a crime in order to hold on to his insulated world.

In *Scarlet Street* the next year, Robinson plays another victim, goaded once again by a bewitching, two-timing woman into becoming a criminal. Robinson's temptress (Joan Bennett) and romantic rival (Dan Duryea) are played by the same actors as in the earlier film; this time all three play coarser versions of their character types. *Scarlet Street* is darker, more brooding than its predecessor, but it's also more blatant.

Robinson has a full-fledged character part as a meek, forlorn clerk (the actor borrows something of his characterization from *The Whole Town's Talking*) who is burdened with a nagging wife and who comforts himself by painting. Through a chance meeting, lowlifer Bennett latches onto him, and she and boyfriend Duryea work the gullible painter for all he's worth. Naïve, put-on Christopher Cross is duped by the two smoothies, but when he's taunted beyond endurance, he kills Bennett. As in *Woman in the Window*, Duryea pays for the crime—the police think he did it. Cross goes free, a broken, shattered man who looks like Little Caesar on the skids and who, ironically, cannot step foward to identify himself as the painter of his own high-priced work.

Because Cross is not prosecuted, the film ran into censorship problems. But the ending is really highly moral; even if he hasn't been caught, Cross is self-convicted. He's a guilt-ridden, useless old man.

As in *Woman in the Window*, Robinson is the hapless victim propelled by a series of ironic coincidences into the role of murderer. Failures as womanizers, both characters begin to slide when they first allow themselves to be tempted by a femme fatale. Enticed by sex, the stolid professor and the mousy clerk become killers. Both parts are unflattering. Robinson is the outsider—the patsy, the sport of the other characters' grim jests. His sexually repressed characters are contrasted to Dan Duryea's tall, trim villains, who slink off to the side waiting to satisfy the wicked heroine's lust.

The roles are very different from the gangsters and the tycoons Robinson had played originally, yet these cowardly victims and makers of wrong decisions are fighters when pushed. Both roles, in fact, have that double-edged quality that always fascinated Robinson. Ignited by extreme circumstances, the stodgy psychology professor has within him the makings of a crafty outlaw; under the meek facade, the painter is capable of a crime of passion. Robinson's homeliness served the parts well—audiences had no trouble seeing him as a hard-luck guy taken in by a beautiful woman, and yet the actor's inevitable scowl hinted at the villainy the characters had in reserve.

Robinson plays a different kind of killer in *All My Sons*. In selling defective airplane parts to the government, Joe Keller is morally responsible for the death of many American soldiers. Based faithfully on Arthur Miller's somber play, the film is a thoroughly intelligent job, and it contains what may well be Robinson's finest performance.

All My Sons is an early treatment of themes that were to concern Miller in most of his subsequent work, particularly *Death of a Salesman* and *The Price*. As in these later works, the focus is a father-son confrontation in which the son becomes progressively disillusioned. Chris Keller (Burt Lancaster), like the Loman brothers in *Death of a Salesman*, ends up rejecting his father's worship of money and status. As he reconstructs the events of the day on which the defective parts were shipped, Chris learns that his father escaped being sent to prison only through a legal technicality. A moral coward and a hypocrite, Joe Keller allowed his partner to take full responsibility for the "crime."

Ignoring his guilt, Joe has pretended for years to be a model business- and family man. At the climax, he learns that his other son, Larry, who has been missing in action, killed himself in shame when he discovered his father's duplicity. Confronted at last by the depth of

ALL MY SONS (1948). With Mady Christians

ALL MY SONS (1948). With Burt Lancaster

his moral bankruptcy, Keller realizes that all the young men who were killed in his planes were symbolically his sons.

The material is patently contrived; the theme is relentless and sermonizing. Arthur Miller is a much too insistent moralist. But *All My Sons*, like *Death of a Salesman*, is a strong drama that dismantles the American dream, and the part of Joe Keller was probably the most fully written role Robinson ever had. As he gets underneath the mask of confidence and good cheer of this self-deceived, fatally compromised American businessman, Robinson is immense. He approaches the character sympathetically. His Keller is not a villain (that's not, after all, the way the character sees himself) but a decent man corrupted by superficial values. Preoccupied with making money as an end in itself, he's a well-meaning man gone wrong. A stubborn fighter who celebrates the Protestant ethic of hard work, he doesn't yield until he's forced to face his responsibility for his son's death. That moment of recognition when he sees, perhaps for the first time, exactly what his values have made him, is Robinson's finest movie moment. As he climbs up the stairs, the lifeblood drained from him, Robinson is moving and human in a way that movies had never let him be before.

Robinson wasn't always the best judge of his own work. He "hastened to finish" *Scarlet Street*, in which he had one of his richest roles, because he thought that both he and the story were monotonous. But Robinson was right about his work in *All My Sons*: "It is a picture of which I am inordinately proud . . . It was a part I played with such passion and intensity that the director, Irving Reis, told me constantly to take it easy . . . my passion imbued the whole cast."* For once, he was playing a role close to home. Miller's drama wasn't about a gang boss, but about a middle-class family man. Robinson identified with Joe Keller in a way he could not identify with all the Little Caesars of the past. An anguished family man in real life, with an estranged, mentally ill wife and a heavily drinking son, he was seldom given the opportunity to play strong domestic drama on screen; when he had scripts like *All My Sons* and *House of Strangers*, in which he portrays a despotic Sicilian patriarch, he acted with enormous strength and conviction.

In order to pay for his paintings, Robinson had to work steadily. Besides, he liked acting and he liked to keep busy. He realized that he couldn't wait around for the big parts, and so he accepted most of

*Robinson, *All My Yesterdays*, p. 253.

what was offered. In the forties, this included supporting roles, roles in omnibus films, and leads in formula pictures. The hard-working professional, Robinson stepped quickly from prestige films to programmers, from star billing to featured player. Sometimes he chose well; sometimes he took what was at hand.

Robinson knew that with his lopsided, craggy looks, he could not always count on getting star parts; he had been lucky as it was. In the forties, he edged into the supporting actor category. In choosing his two major featured parts, he was fortunate; as the persistent insurance investigator in *Double Indemnity* (1944) and as the equally determined pursuer of Nazis in *The Stranger* (1946), he had rewarding roles in which his supporting actor status was almost concealed.

For both parts, Robinson was squarely on the right side of the law. Both times he was once again a man without a family, a man wholly committed to—in fact, lost in—his job. These Robinson bachelors and staunch defenders of morality are single-minded almost to the point of mania.

Billy Wilder's *Double Indemnity* is one of the classic *films noirs* of the decade. With a screenplay by Wilder and Raymond Chandler (based on a novel by James M. Cain), the film is typical of its director's cynical view of American values. "It's a movie," wrote Bosley Crowther in the *Times*, "designed plainly to freeze the marrow in an audience's bones . . . it's hard and inflexible as steel." The conspirators—an insurance man and a two-timing wife—are motivated almost solely by greed; though sex distracts them for a while, they murder the woman's husband mostly for the insurance money.

Barbara Stanwyck, as the conniving, cold-blooded temptress, and Fred MacMurray, as the easily corruptible insurance man, dominate Wilder's swift and trenchant melodrama. But, in a distinctly secondary part, Robinson almost walks away with the movie. He hadn't snapped out his lines so authoritatively, or curled his lip so threateningly, or used his hands so expressively, since his heyday in the early thirties. He makes the investigator a genuine original—an eccentric, dyspeptic office joke who's the toughest, sharpest guy in his business, a claims man with remarkable insights into the criminal mind. With him in pursuit, the clever conspirators are doomed.

His acting in Orson Welles' film, *The Stranger*, is as subdued as his work in *Double Indemnity* is extroverted. In order to investigate a suspected Nazi who's hiding out in a small Connecticut town, Robinson poses as a very mild-mannered an-

DOUBLE INDEMNITY (1944). With Fred MacMurray

tique collector. (The role was originally intended for Agnes Moorehead.) As in his other Nazi-hunter role, in *Confessions of a Nazi Spy,* Robinson is the straight man. The showpiece parts belong to the men he pursues with such tireless zeal. Here, while Robinson quietly asks questions and ponders answers (it's a thoughtful, selfless performance), the emoting is done by Welles himself, as the Nazi in hiding, and Loretta Young, as his innocent new bride. Playing an impassioned crackpot, Welles bulldozes his way through the part; he isn't really convincing as a Nazi or as the teacher in a boys' school that the character pretends to be, but he offers his standard baroque performance.

Though the role of investigator is one of Robinson's masquerade parts, it's not as ambiguous and complex as it might be. Robinson, however, plays it with a dry humor, and his solid presence counters Welles' sometimes operatic excesses as actor and director. Quietly smoking his pipe, sedately drinking

DOUBLE INDEMNITY (1944). With Barbara Stanwyck and Fred MacMurray

THE STRANGER (1946). As Wilson

LARCENY, INC. (1942). With Edward Brophy

coffee, patiently explaining to Young the situation she's in, and playing a sly, teasing game with Welles, Robinson gives the film the firm center it needs.

The Stranger is Welles' least popular film. Welles himself dismisses it, and so does Robinson. But the film has a quietly sinister atmosphere that's very effective, and it's filled with eccentric touches that only a master director could invent. (The most bizarre: the villainous Nazi meets his end impaled on the sword of a revolving metal figure on the town's huge clock.)

Robinson's star parts in minor films were much less rewarding. Many of the films, of course, contained reprises of previous roles. As a con man masquerading as a monk in *Brother Orchid* (1940), and as a mobster just out of Sing Sing trying hard to go straight in *Larceny, Inc.* (1942), Robinson added to his gallery of comic gangsters. In *Unholy Partners* (1941), he was another hard-nosed, muckraking journalist. Robinson's sinister presence is called upon in *The Red House* (1947), in which he's a farmer haunted by guilt for a past misdeed; in *Night*

Has a Thousand Eyes (1948), in which he's a doomed crystal-ball gazer; and in *Flesh and Fantasy* (1943), in which he's an eminent lawyer who's told by a fortune-teller that he will commit murder.

In some of his programmers, though, Robinson did manage to escape hard-core type-casting. In *Destroyer* (1943), he's a gabby, slightly unhinged ship's captain who commands according to the old school and who proves more courageous than any of his younger sailors. In *Tampico* (1944), he is another sea captain, but this time his usual hard-boiled character is chastened by love. In *Tales of Manhattan* (1942), he's an educated bum who is regenerated when he goes to a class reunion in a discarded full-dress suit.

For *Mr. Winkle Goes to War* (1944), in which he plays a milquetoast thrown into the army, Robinson borrowed again his namby-pamby clerk in *The Whole Town's Talking*, but he was still too strong for what the part really required. As happened often when he tried to change his act, critics didn't fully accept the "new" Robinson.

THE RED HOUSE (1947). With Judith Anderson

NIGHT HAS A THOUSAND EYES (1948). As John Triton

TALES OF MANHATTAN (1942). With James Gleason and Mae Marsh

His transformation into the bumbling Mr. Winkle looked too much like a half-hearted stunt. "Somehow his granite-chiseled visage and his plainly hard-boiled voice betray a contradiction which insistently muddles his act," wrote Bosley Crowther. "It is hard to believe that Mr. Robinson would take what he does lying down."*

Robinson's best programmer of the decade was *Manpower* (1941), directed by Raoul Walsh. Here, in another romantic triangle (the film was patterned on *Tiger Shark*), the homely Robinson was the sure loser. Robinson and George Raft are buddies who have a dangerous job as linemen who repair telephone wires. Raft is Johnny Marshall, the cool ladies' man, confident of his sex appeal. Robinson, more human and vulnerable, is the good-natured, gullible victim. His Hank McHenry is crazy about women, but the guy just doesn't have Johnny's touch. We first see Robinson dancing wildly across a crowded floor in a

---

*The New York Times, August, 1944.

MR. WINKLE GOES TO WAR (1944). As Wilbert G. Winkle

MANPOWER (1941). With Ward Bond (being restrained) and George Raft

rundown bar, smiling too broadly and holding onto his dame too tightly. One look and we know he's never going to make it.

In a masculine environment, on the job with men or enjoying some beers at the local bar, Hank knows how to get along. But when it comes to women, he's no operator. When Fay Duval (Marlene Dietrich), an alluring woman with a shady past, enters his life, he's a goner. Fay marries him, even though she never says she loves him, when all the time it's Johnny, aloof and sure of himself, who entices her. The triangle concludes, inevitably, with Hank conveniently dying, thereby giving the womanly woman to her rightful partner, the manly man.

Robinson's is a generous role, moving as it does from broad comedy to pathos. At first, we're encouraged to laugh at his awkward and hopeless lineman, but we end up respecting him. The story is familiar, but the working-class background is colorfully detailed, and Robinson and Dietrich are a remarkably edgy romantic duo.

HOUSE OF STRANGERS (1949). As Gino Monetti

What would Little Caesar have done with Dietrich? Robinson's modest workingman here can only regard her with reverence and awe—she's his deliverance. Robinson had never had such a glamorous leading lady before, and he doesn't know quite what to do with her. Both performers are much too big for their roles (as a restless hausfrau in a backwoods town, Dietrich is rather preposterous). But Robinson thought the two of them were "a stunning combination. Our joint presence was tough box office."*

*Robinson, *All My Yesterdays*, p. 221.

The forties was Robinson's most productive decade. He was never again to get such meaty roles, or to appear in major films of major directors. The dividing line between major and minor Robinson, between Robinson the star and Robinson the old-timer, the remnant from an earlier era in films, was the blacklist. By the end of the forties, the actor was unemployable in Hollywood. Listed in *Red Channels* as a Communist sympathizer, he was ostracized by an industry which he had served continuously for twenty years. Robinson ended the major phase of his career in 1948 with a banner year—*Key Largo, House of Strangers, All My Sons*. In 1949 he had only a cameo role in a Doris Day musical, *It's a Great Feeling*. Playing himself—or, more accurately—the tough guy that audiences identified him with, he said that he would do anything to keep working at his job. It was an ominous preview of the next few years, when he couldn't get work.

He vigorously fought the Communist charge. The evidence against him consisted of his contributions to organizations that had proven Communist ties. A known philanthropist and soft touch, Robinson was often approached by organizations, and he gave generously, without always knowing exactly what he was giving to. After much time in court, and several trips to Washington to defend himself before congressional committees, Robinson won total exoneration.

The charges had been especially wounding because Robinson always considered himself an exemplary American. In October, 1947, he told a congressional committee: "I think I have not only been a good citizen. I think I have been an extraordinarily good citizen and I value this above everything else . . . I think I may have taken money under false pretenses in my own business, and I may not have been as good a husband or father or friend as I should have been, but I know my Americanism is unblemished and fine and wonderful, and I am proud of it, and I don't feel it is conceit on my part to say this, and I stand on my record or fall on it."*

*Robinson, *All My Yesterdays*, p. 263.

ROBINSON IN THE FIFTIES: KEEPING BUSY IN A LEAN TIME

When Robinson returned to full-time filmmaking in 1953, his standing was very different from what it had been in the old days at First National and as a high-ranking free-lance in the forties. In 1948 Robinson had been a star; by 1953 he was an old-timer, the product of a tight studio system and stock company tradition that was already on the verge of disintegration. In the early fifties, in short, Robinson was considered a has-been; producers had forgotten that only a few years before he had given some of his strongest performances. From 1953 to 1956 Robinson was offered a series of modest black-and-white second features of the sort that Hollywood stopped making by the end of the decade. Eager to return to work under any conditions, he accepted ordinary material, his self-respect diminishing further after each assignment had been completed.

Robinson had taken up the slack in 1951-52—when he hadn't been offered any parts at all—by returning to the stage for the first time in twenty years. He starred in the second company of *Darkness at Noon*, re-creating Claude Rains' original Broadway role. Robinson hoped that an extensive tour in a demanding role would reestablish his reputation. The role made a political statement for the actor as well: in playing an old-line Communist who is rejected by the new regime and who in turn rejects the party, Robinson hoped to erase any lingering doubts about his own politics. When he signed for the tour, Robinson told the press: "I consider this play a most important instrument in the struggle against Communism. The struggle has reached such a point that it is no longer enough simply to take sides verbally . . . the basic issue is one of human freedom, and the rights of man are at stake in this conflict."

The role paralleled Robinson's recent professional history too: Rubashov was a grand old man who had lost his standing. The character's gentlemanly Old World manner is sharply contrasted to the ruthless young men who have gained control of the party. Rubashov's idealism is opposed throughout to the cynical and demented young general who is in charge of the prison.

A fatherly victim of terrorist forces, Rubashov is a sympathetic role. It's a rigorous role too: the character is on stage at all times; scenes from the past that recount

THE GLASS WEB (1953). With Kathleen Hughes

ILLEGAL (1955). With Nina Foch

his rise in the party and that recreate the kind of loyalty he was once able to inspire, are interspersed with details of Rubashov's present confinement as he awaits execution.

Darkness at Noon is a schematic play in which characters represent political positions, but it allowed Robinson a chance to portray a figure of dignity. And the tour accomplished what Robinson had wanted: it helped to silence the Communist accusations, and it reminded people that he was still a powerful and usable actor.

The movie roles that began to come in after the tour ended in 1952 hardly matched the scope of Arthur Koestler's tortured, beleaguered hero. From *Vice Squad* in 1953 to *Hell on Frisco Bay* in 1956, the films were strictly lower-case items in which Robinson played his usual assortment of detectives, lawyers, investigators, outlaws, and madmen. Whether on the right side of the law or not, he was usually cast as the Boss. For a change of pace, he appeared as the training camp coach of the New York Giants in *The Big Leaguer*

(1953), but the rest of the time guns and criminals were the order of the day.

He is a good guy in *Tight Spot* (1955) as a federal agent who tries to protect a key witness (Ginger Rogers) from a crime czar's killers, and in *Nightmare* (1956) as a homicide detective. But the actor, characteristically, made a sharper impression when he played devious types. In *The Glass Web* (1953), he murders a beautiful blonde who's given him the air and he concocts a clever scheme by which to implicate a colleague at a television station. In *Black Tuesday* (1954), he is a Death Row resident who escapes, only to be killed in the inevitable shootout. In *Illegal* (1955), he plays a wheeler-dealer lawyer who switches from the right side to the wrong side of the law and then reverts to nobility in the end.

In "Actor's Blood," the first segment of *Actors and Sin* (1952), he has another masquerade part. As in *The Man With Two Faces* twenty years earlier, he plays an eminent actor who applies his talent for transformation to a real-life situation. The egomaniacal actor in this two-part Ben Hecht film gave Robinson the kind of stellar role he always sought.

The old, snappy, flamboyant Robinson was clearly in evidence, however, in his two splashiest vehicles of this period: in *The Violent Men* (1955) and *Hell on Frisco Bay* (1956), the actor was as surly and ornery as ever. The material plainly lacked the punch of the vintage Robinson films, but in these two late performances the actor demonstrated something of the old size and bite.

In *The Violent Men*, in which Robinson's tough guy exploded in a Western for the first time, the actor is paired with Barbara Stanwyck as two of the meanest landowners who ever ruled the range. As Robinson's vicious wife, carrying on an affair with ranch foreman Brian Keith, Stanwyck offers an all-out reprise of her bad-woman routine from *Double Indemnity*, and Robinson growls with evident pleasure as the avaricious, crippled empire builder she tries (but fails) to destroy in a climactic fire.

In *Hell On Frisco Bay*, Robinson plays a dock czar who rubs out his own nephew. Robinson's performance is ebullient; the actor had finally latched onto a role that was as meaty as some of his best parts, and he wasn't afraid to risk self-parody. He has some wonderfully nasty dialogue, and in the movie's most expansive scene, he and Fay Wray have a shouting match. "You're nothing but a broken-down, has-been broad," he snarls at her. "Get out of here, you filthy peasant," the woman rejoins. "A slob like you, calling me

BLACK TUESDAY (1954). As Vincent Canelli

THE VIOLENT MEN (1955). With Barbara Stanwyck, Brian Keith, and Glenn Ford

names," Robinson spits out at her, "a washed-up dame in love with a guy with a twisted face!" Alan Ladd was the hero, but it was Robinson's movie.

Critics were delighted. "Even after all these years," wrote William Zinsser in the *New York Herald Tribune* (January 7, 1956), "Robinson is a fascinating boss, in his pearl gray homburg and gray silk vest, glaring out of slitted eyes at a man he is soon to kill, flicking the ashes of an expensive cigar nonchalantly on the rug. His commands are edged with a sardonic wit, and he is quick to give the girl the back of his hand if she spurns his silky advances. This is the old meanie at the top of his form, relishing every black minute of his role."

Except for these two explosive characterizations, for which Robinson opened all the stops, the actor was restrained during this minor

HELL ON FRISCO BAY (1956). With Paul Stewart and Fay Wray

phase of his career. He underplayed, giving his standard roles no more than they deserved, but he also discovered a subtler and more relaxed style than he had ever had before. In routine assignments in films like *Illegal*, *Tight Spot*, and *A Bullet for Joey*, the pressure clearly was off, and Robinson, the erstwhile scenery-chewer, became a more natural and uninflected actor; he was the coolest old-timer in town, drolly underacting his way through a string of second features.

Robinson's new style is especially effective in *Vice Squad* (1953) and *A Bullet for Joey* (1955). The former, which details a day in the life of a harried Los Angeles detective, is early fifties *Dragnet* transferred to the big screen. Robinson is a no-nonsense professional surrounded by an array of B-movie kooks and loonies: a fake Italian count; a smart-talking madam; a Walter Mitty type who's witnessed a killing and is afraid to talk, because it will expose his ex-

VICE SQUAD (1953). With Porter Hall

A BULLET FOR JOEY (1955). With George Dolenz

tramarital affair with a floozy; a man who's pursued by shadows; a smarmy television interviewer. Throughout his encounters with these unstrung characters, Robinson remains the wry, observant questioner. The supporting character actors work their few moments for comedy and color; Robinson, smoking his pipe, folding his hands on his vest, his face frozen in a perpetual frown that implies a kind of sour patience, is the straight man. With a withering glance, a slow look of amazement, a flick of his wrist, Robinson distances himself from distraught clients, incompetent underlings, and sleazy suspects. His scenes with Paulette Goddard as the madam have a nice teasing ring; they're two old pros on holiday, having quiet fun with their stock parts. Typically, though Robinson's detective is married, we never go home with him; he's a grimly efficient sleuth, and our

A BULLET FOR JOEY (1955).
With George Raft

THE TEN COMMANDMENTS (1956). With Yul Brynner

business with him includes only the nine-to-five part of his day.

Robinson plays the same kind of part in *A Bullet for Joey*; once again he's the clever man of the law, sardonic, impersonal, probing. This time he pursues George Raft, and the pairing, in the mid-fifties, of these two thirties tough guys, gives the film some added mileage. Their roles here prove (as if proof were needed) that Robinson had the greater versatility and humanity, whereas Raft continued to be the second-rate, unlikable tough guy.

With Raft cast as the old-time public enemy trying for a comeback, and Robinson as the individualist who expels the contaminating hood and his gang, *A Bullet for Joey* is something of a B-movie *Key Largo*. Raft and his cronies are called back from retirement for one last gig. Replaying his standard, hard-as-nails con man, Raft represents the old-style criminal, while his cohorts, and especially his moll, are very much lower-case fifties hoods. The film therefore has a curious schizoid streak, thirties movie bad guys from the great tradition mingling uneasily with public enemies from a later and of course much blander movie era.

That the gang is in the employ of Russians, and that their goal is to kidnap a nuclear scientist, gives the film cold war political overtones. Faced with the task of cracking the gang, Robinson is again cast as the determined foe of Communists: in the final confrontation, he argues Raft into a heroic act of turning against his employers. Like Bogart in *Key Largo*, Robinson becomes the agent who rids the world of a symbolically charged criminal conspiracy.

Robinson worked steadily from 1953 to 1956, turning in solid, craftsmanlike performances; he was never less than professional during this low period. In a few cases—as his droll, underdone self in *Vice Squad*, and as his explosive, manic self in *Hell On Frisco Bay*—he was almost as forceful as he had ever been. But there were too many undistinguished entries, and though he was always starred, Robinson was no longer considered a player of the first rank.

He thought that his real chance for professional vindication came when Cecil B. DeMille offered him the role of Dathan in *The Ten Commandments*. In the inflated atmosphere that surrounded the making of his epic, the director announced to the press that the part he was offering Robinson would be the greatest of the actor's career. Robinson allowed himself to be at least a little persuaded by the rhetoric, and in his autobiography he cites the film as his return to major filmmaking: "The top directors and producers wouldn't have me and while I'm grateful to those who did in the period and bow low to them for their guts, what I needed was recognition again by a top figure in the industry . . . Cecil B. DeMille returned me to films. Cecil B. DeMille restored my self-respect."*

Though its stilted direction often seems antique, *The Ten Commandments* has undeniable epic sweep. The story of Moses was shaped to cater to a mass popular audience, and as a lavish, simplified verson of biblical events, the film has a strong, if crude, appeal; it even has dignity. But for Robinson the assignment afforded no triumph. Clearly ill-at-ease in his abbreviated costume, he acts in a stiff, declamatory manner and his

*Robinson, *All My Yesterdays*, p.212.

THE TEN COMMANDMENTS (1956). As Dathan

A HOLE IN THE HEAD (1959). With Thelma Ritter and Frank Sinatra

performance as the self-serving Hebrew overseer who is a traitor to his people may well be the poorest of his long career. The film was Robinson's first spectacle and playing an ancient Hebrew, Robinson seems inescapably like a modern, big-city operator. Perhaps he had too much personality for his part; most of the other actors were protected by their blandness. Scowling on the sidelines, pointing rhetorically to the heavens as he denounces the Hebrew god who has forsaken his people, playing up the role of the traditional skeptic and naysayer, the actor was working in a patently alien milieu. In ancient Egypt and on the parched desert sands, Robinson was far from home.

After *The Ten Commandments*, Robinson left movies and returned to the theater for the kind of challenge and gratification that Hollywood wasn't offering. This time he opened a show on Broadway. As Paddy Chayesfsky's middle-aged businessman in *Middle of the Night*, he had a congenial role. The part extended the mellow, low-key

Robinson that had graced the likes of *Vice Squad*, and it gave him the chance to do domestic rather than crime drama.

As the Queens widower who falls in love with a woman young enough to be his daughter, Robinson was playing another of Chayefsky's troubled "little" people. The play is written in the author's distinctive brand of small talk; though seemingly realistic, the dialogue has an insistent, almost incantatory rhythm: the repetitions, the fragments, the backtrackings, the endlessly extended sentences, approach self-parody. But the playwright's ear is accurate, and his drama abounds in little shocks of recognition. Robinson attacked the subtly stylized dialogue with a quiet power far removed from his high-flying vaudeville star turns of old.

Playing in an uncharacteristic domestic milieu, Robinson excised all traces of the Boss from his portrayal. As Jerry Kingsley, the lonely widower who finds a second chance for love, he enacted the decent, hard-working character that studio publicity often claimed was the real-life Robinson. He was the untainted family figure, a character who was not, for a change, larger than life. Here he played, at last, a sympathetic middle-class Jewish character instead of the assortment of unsavory Italians and Greeks that the movies often reserved for him.

After his professional vindication in *Middle of the Night* in 1956, Robinson didn't work again until *A Hole in the Head* in 1959. As in Chayefsky's play, he was an archetypal middle-class ethnic New Yorker, exponent of a hard-working, penny-pinching, immigrant ethic. To accommodate the star, Frank Sinatra, Robinson was nominally playing an Italian, but the character was unmistakably Jewish, a stock Jewish tradesman, in fact, a kibitzer and a nonstop worker saddled with a haranguing wife, a nebbish son, and a no-good brother. A constant complainer, the Robinson character is soft as marshmallow underneath; though he's tight-fisted, he loosens up whenever he's handed a sob story.

Robinson is the straight brother, the good brother; Sinatra is the high-liver. For Robinson, it's work and responsibility; for Sinatra, it's dames and booze. Sinatra is the breezy Damon Runyon guy to Robinson's Jewish Babbitt.

A Hole in the Head, directed by Frank Capra in his best heartwarming manner, contains one of Robinson's finest comedy performances. He and Thelma Ritter, as the well-meaning, interfering, tactless in-laws, easily dominate the movie as they try to convert the free-living Sinatra to their straight and narrow way of life. They want Frank to settle down in a nice, steady little business with a nice, steady little woman. Sinatra's way wins, and Robinson and Ritter take the first vacation of their lives, running barefoot along the Miami beachfront.

Robinson's flair for the barbed line and the sarcastic grimace was never brushed with such an airy touch—this is the actor's lightest and perhaps most graceful performance. The scenes in which he and Ritter hector the misbehaving Sinatra are models of deft comic timing, and Robinson's misfortunes with a collapsible chair provide a beautiful vaudeville turn. Unfortunately, Robinson never had the chance to do this Yiddish theater kind of work again—seeing him with Molly Picon in a lightweight Second Avenue comedy of manners would indeed have been a treat.

THE LAST YEARS

During his minor period in the early fifties, Robinson was still the star, but after 1956, he was inevitably a supporting player, a guest star, a grand old man. Whether he played criminals or statesmen, Robinson in the sixties was wise and grandfatherly. Looking weathered, he was more mellow than he had ever been before: he was a movie veteran, remote and magisterial. The films in which he appeared used him as a link to earlier film cycles; in *Robin and the Seven Hoods* (1964), a farce version of the roaring twenties gang world, he plays a boss who's shot down at a testimonial dinner, and his presence connects the film to the old crime sagas.

Like *Robin and the Seven Hoods*, the actor's gang movies in the sixties were parodies, light comedies, or flimsy thrillers, altogether lacking the social comment and the dynamism of the classic Robinsons. In these anemic films, the tag end of a movie tradition, Robinson was used for his lordly, commanding presence; he was an icon that recalled the heyday of the gangster movie, and his appearance alone gave the tired little caper films some small share in the glory of a great movie heritage.

Robinson's typical role in the sixties was that of the criminal mastermind. In *Seven Thieves* (1960), *The Biggest Bundle of Them All* (1968), *Grand Slam* (1968), and *Never a Dull Moment* (1968), he is the brains behind a robbery. He's the man with the idea, the respected old-timer who wants to plan one final caper. Robinson plays the godfather who's available for advice but who's too old now to carry out his schemes by himself. Bleary-eyed and a little slow, he entrusts the heavy work to youngsters.

In these late crime films, Robinson is a sedate behind-the-scenes operator rather than an aggressive front-runner. He plays characters who have fought most of their battles and who, though they still run a tight ship, have a detachment that Little Caesar couldn't afford. The old con man looks at his younger colleagues and at the straight world at large with the rueful wisdom that comes with age.

Grand Slam, in which Robinson is not a retired mobster but a schoolteacher who has planned for years to rob the bank across from the school he has dutifully served, is at least exciting, our interest maintained by clever plot twists. But *The Biggest Bundle of Them All* is a limp mixture of comedy and thrills (though Robinson gets to do the twist with Raquel Welch), and

GRAND SLAM (1968). With Janet Leigh

Seven Thieves is totally flaccid. Detailing a clever scheme to rob the casino at Monte Carlo, the film is dull, but it offers some interesting comparisons among its actors. Robinson is the leader of an outfit that includes Rod Steiger and Eli Wallach, and it's instructive to see how these three mannered tough guys handle their roles. In the caper, Wallach plays a petty, autocratic German baron while Robinson masquerades as his physician. Wallach overdoes it, sputtering and stammering so histrionically that he almost ruins the charade. Robinson underacts in his late droll manner, tossing off his lines as the fake doctor with just the right tart quality. If Wallach overworks the flimsy material, Steiger, evidently bored, gives nothing at all. Occasionally he erupts into one of his typical rantings, but the explosions have no connection to his role here. Only

NEVER A DULL MOMENT (1968). With Dick Van Dyke

THE BIGGEST BUNDLE OF THEM ALL (1968). With Vittorio De Sica

Robinson gives the proper professional gloss to his work.

In almost all of his sixties movies, Robinson plays venerated old-timers. He's not always a crook and he's not always top man in big city settings, but Robinson was typically cast as an eminent figure, a man of substance and integrity whatever his profession. In *My Geisha* (1962), he is an understanding film producer. In *The Prize* (1964), he is a world-renowned scientist who disappears mysteriously during the Nobel Prize ceremonies in Stockholm. In *Good Neighbor Sam* (1964), he is a moralistic business tycoon. In *Song of Norway* (1970), he appears as a prosperous piano merchant who is also a musical connoisseur. (The part was a variation on his real-life role of art collector.) Even as a grizzled prospector with a secret horde of gold in *Mackenna's Gold* (1969), or as a shaggy diamond smuggler who resembled Hemingway in *A Boy Ten Feet Tall* (1965), Robinson was allowed the kind of stature that only a distinguished movie veteran could claim.

In his last role, in *Soylent Green* (1973), Robinson plays an embittered old man who clings to civilized values in an overcrowded city of the science fiction future. Robinson's role, suggested Paul Zimmerman in *Newsweek* (May 7, 1973), is "a parody of the last cultured man. He sports a beret, caresses old books, listens to light classical music and dreams of the old days when men were men." Though the character doesn't hold out against the barbarism of the ecological wasteland and ultimately gives himself up to a suicide center, Robinson plays him with heroic dignity.

In this last phase of his career, Robinson more than ever turned unlikable characters into intermittently sympathetic figures. The edge was removed from most of his performances, and even in nasty parts he acted with statesmanlike reserve. Drawing on their fond memories of his past work, audiences responded warmly to Robinson regardless of the characters he played. Little Caesar had become a Buddha-like grandfather who was likable despite the sometimes sour demeanor. One of the actor's most compelling qualities in the old days had been exactly his ability to be both menacing and fatherly at the same time; there had always been a human side to even the most notorious of his lunatics. Now, in old age, Robinson's instinctive warmth dominated, even in his infrequent roles as heavies.

As written, his characters in *The Outrage* (1964) and *Two Weeks in Another Town* (1962) are cynics and phonies. But Robinson performs with a sincerity that softens the

*SEVEN THIEVES (1960).
As Theo Wilkins*

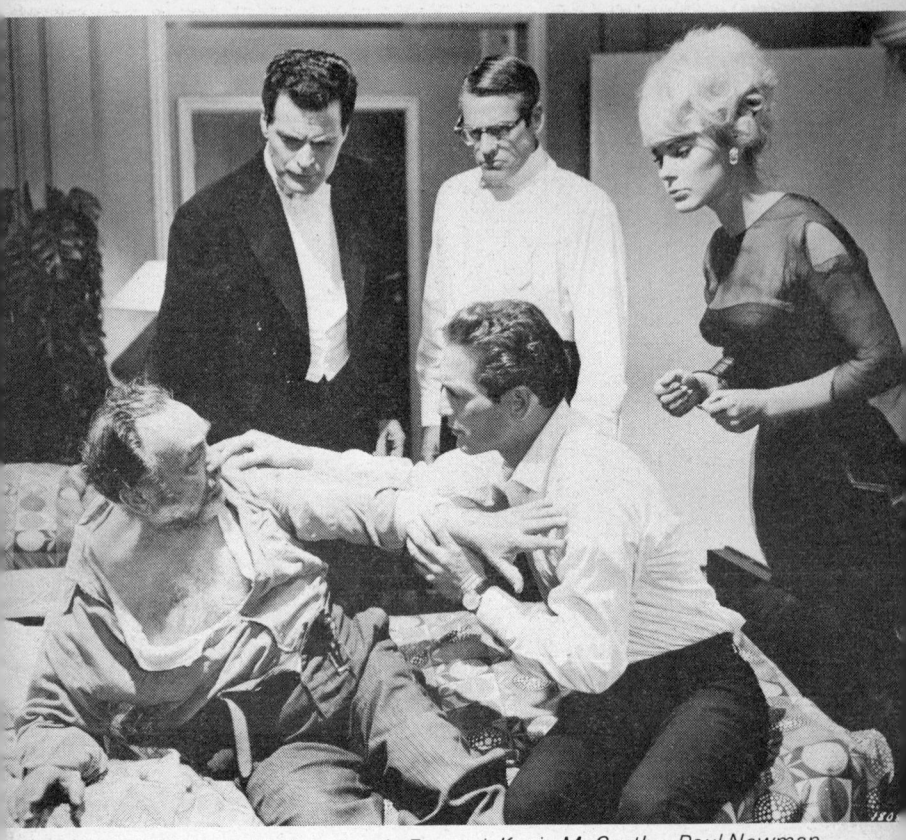

THE PRIZE (1964). With Sergio Fantoni, Kevin McCarthy, Paul Newman, and Elke Sommer

characters' sharp edges. In *The Outrage*, a Western version of *Rashomon*, directed by Martin Ritt, he is a small-time con man who listens to different versions of the same story involving a notorious Mexican outlaw, a confederate colonel, and the colonel's wife, and who doesn't believe any of the versions. Playing a professional doubting Thomas who speaks for a narrow, black vision of human nature, Robinson delivers his speeches to a priest and a prospector with a neat oratorical flourish. At the end, the priest and the prospector form an alliance after they've been transformed by discovering an abandoned baby in a darkened corner of the railroad station in which they

McKENNA'S GOLD (1969). As Old Adams

A BOY TEN FEET TALL (1965). With Fergus McClelland

have waited out a storm. Robinson, however, remains the demonic tempter. He beckons to the prospector to join him on the train that's arriving at the station, but the man chooses the baby and the priest —chooses life over the negative, skeptical attitude that Robinson's character expresses.

The attempt to transfer *Rashomon* to the American West was strained, but Robinson's grizzled nonbeliever is one of the strongest performances of his last decade. He transforms his two-bit cynic into a wiser and more sensitive character than the film's scheme calls for.

Robinson humanized another cretin in *Two Weeks in Another Town*, a shrill Hollywood-on-Hollywood movie directed by Vincente Minnelli. Like *Sunset Boulevard*, of which it is but a pale

THE OUTRAGE (1964). As the Con Man

TWO WEEKS IN ANOTHER TOWN (1962). With Kirk Douglas and Claire Trevor

echo, the film is about has-beens aiming for a comeback. Robinson plays a once-famed director reduced to working on tawdry Italian quickies, and Kirk Douglas is a once-popular leading man who has cracked up.

It's a bitter portrait of movie colony sluttishness in which Robinson is a dyspeptic hatchet man who pretends to have a heart. Taunting the shaky Douglas, cringing before amoral Italian moneymen, humiliating his wretched wife (Claire Trevor), Robinson stomps full steam ahead through one of his most bravura parts during his last twenty years in movies.

With its colorful behind-the-scenes glimpses of moviemaking,

TWO WEEKS IN ANOTHER TOWN (1962). With Claire Trevor

its Via Veneto sleaziness, and its self-flagellating characters, *Two Weeks in Another Town* is glittering trash in which only Robinson and Trevor transcend the meretricious script. The most pointed scenes (with their echoes of *Key Largo* and even *The Amazing Dr. Clitterhouse*) are between these two seasoned actors. Robinson again plays the sadist to Trevor's masochist, and in one of her last performances to date, Trevor goes all out as Robinson's twitchy harridan of a wife. She is especially virulent as she tells off a disintegrating Kirk Douglas: "You're crazy," she screeches at full blast, "and you ought to go back to the nut house where you belong!"

Robinson matches Trevor's vulgarity with his withering, bone-crunching sarcasm. Enacting two monumentally unpleasant characters, Robinson and his old-time leading lady are glorious. But even here he manages to inject some human touches. He indicates the fear that underlies his director's comeback attempt and he suggests the kind of twisted loyalty that makes him stay with Trevor despite their colossal battles. In one scene he breaks down in his wife's arms, and Robinson cries with such intensity that we are given a whole new view of the character. He makes the script's flat character round and complex.

The best of Robinson's elder statesmen roles (the roles that contained tributes to the actor both for himself and for the kinds of parts he played in films) were in *Cheyenne Autumn* (1964) and *The Cincinnati Kid* (1965). Both parts required the presence of a famous and respected actor. In *The Cincinnati Kid*, Robinson plays the Man, an undefeated poker champ. In John Ford's *Cheyenne Autumn* (in a role originally intended for Spencer Tracy), he is the Secretary of the Interior who settles the dispute between the Indians and the government. He plays both roles with a serenity that comes from forty years on the job.

The sympathetic Secretary was only a cameo, but Robinson plays it with great decorum. In a memorable scene, faced with the problem of the Cheyenne, who have been betrayed by the government and who have embarked on a heroic trek to their homeland, the character looks at a picture of Abraham Lincoln and asks, "What would you do, old friend? What would you do?" John Ford is clearly trying to link his character to Lincoln, and Robinson makes the man grand enough to sustain the comparison.

The Cincinnati Kid, directed by Norman Jewison, is a more characteristic homage to Robinson. Here, in a role that parallels Jackie Gleason's Minnesota Fats in *The Hustler*, Robinson is the champ who

CHEYENNE AUTUMN (1964). As Secretary of the Interior Carl Schurz

THE CINCINNATI KID (1965). As Lancey Howard

THE CINCINNATI KID (1965). With Steve McQueen, Ann-Margret, Karl Malden, and Joan Blondell

defends his title against a young challenger (Steve McQueen). Like all the actor's valedictory characters, Robinson's Lancey Howard has made his peace with the world. He's a self-contained, elegant old gentleman who smokes the finest tobacco, drinks coffee from the choicest china, wears impeccably tailored suits and vests and dressing gowns, stays at the most luxurious hotels, and is accustomed to the most attentive and discreet service. The film points a contrast between Robinson's Old World gentleman and McQueen's new style sharpshooter—the Kid lives in a grimy rooming house, has persistent woman trouble, is rootless, hostile, alienated.

Robinson was proud of his performance; he recognized it, quite

THE CINCINNATI KID (1965). With Steve McQueen

properly, as the finest work he'd done since the forties: "I could hardly say I identified with Lancey; I *was* Lancey. That man on the screen, more than in any other picture I ever made, was Edward G. Robinson with great patches of Emanuel Goldenberg showing through. He was all cold and discerning and unflappable on the exterior; he was aging and full of self-doubt on the inside . . . It was one of the best performances I ever gave . . . and the reason for it is that it wasn't a performance at all; it was symbolically the playing out of my whole gamble with life."*

The Man is another guest star part, in essence, and Robinson has to create a sense of the character through some quick brush strokes: a sardonic glance, a raised eyebrow, a brusque gesture. Much of the performance, especially in the climactic poker game, is silent; the drama is contained in the actors' eyes.

The interesting casting, in which old-timers like Robinson and Joan Blondell mingle with newcomers like McQueen and Ann-Margret, supports the script's contrast between age and youth. Robinson is paired with Blondell, who plays a card dealer named Ladyfingers. Blondell is brilliant. As she and the Man reminisce about players and dealers from the old days, as they exchange cracks and witticisms, they inevitably recall Warners in the thirties. These two old pros perform with a fullness that isn't available to the younger actors; we bring to their work memories of their performances ranging over thirty years, and that knowledge adds dimension to the characters they play here. Robinson and Blondell are too honest to milk those memories for an easy nostalgia, or for cheap shortcuts into their characters, but the movie tradition they represent embellishes their work, and their vivid and even noble presences give the movie its elegiac underpinning.

Steve McQueen was just beginning at the time to develop (successfully) his brand of antihero, Ann-Margret and Tuesday Weld are both very good as, respectively, a tramp and an innocent, the New Orleans setting is mined for exotic atmosphere, but it's Robinson and Blondell who give the movie its real distinction, who make it seem more important than *The Hustler* — imitation that it essentially is.

Robinson's Lancey Howard certainly has all the trimmings of a valedictory role: at the end he proves himself the Champ. As he finally tells McQueen, "You're good, Kid, but as long as I'm around, you'll be second-best."

Robinson, the professional craftsman, never gave a bad per-

*Robinson. *All My Yesterdays*, p. 189.

SOYLENT GREEN (1973). With Charlton Heston

formance, but, like most actors with strong personalities, he often relied on mannerisms and on what the public came to expect of him. When the part was familiar, the actor fell back on doing a Robinson turn, repeating his effects, giving to routine scripts no more than they deserved. Robinson on film was often in the business of merchandising personality—he marketed himself shrewdly, but his work did not always have the kind of continuing exploration and chance-taking that he always seemed capable of but that the studio system and marketplace considerations denied him.

Though he had one of the longest and busiest and most favorably reviewed records in Hollywood history, Robinson's career was finally incomplete and imperfect. For every *Sea Wolf* or *All My Sons* or *Woman in the Window*, there were three or four self-imitations in ordinary films, and for all his attempts to expand his image there were finally too many gangsters and crooks.

For over forty years, Hollywood found a place for this most unhandsome of actors, but it also exploited him and withheld from him the chance to test himself in the great roles. Theater-trained, Robinson had the makings of a classical actor; he would have been a remarkable Lear; and Macbeth, Prospero, Richard III, Ibsen's Master Builder, Chekhov's Uncle Vanya, and Brecht's Galileo, among many others, were surely not beyond him.

Robinson's work contained suggestions of a protean versatility, an Olivier-like genius for transforming himself anew for each role. He gave every indication of being a genuine actor, capable of losing himself in a wide variety of parts. Yet it is one of the ironies of his career that movies often used him more for his star presence than for the infinitely resourceful and chameleon-like character actor he seemed capable of being.

A few weeks before his death in January 1973, the Academy of Motion Picture Arts and Sciences made it up to Robinson for never having nominated him for an award by presenting him with an honorary Oscar for his long and exceptional contribution to films. The award paid proper recognition to a strong and in many ways extraordinary career, but is it possible that if there had never been a *Little Caesar* that career might have been less stellar and well-paying, but finally more varied, more brilliant?

We will never know. Yet he left behind a string of vivid performances, and the memory of his dynamic presence.

BIBLIOGRAPHY

Agee, James. *Agee on Film*. Beacon Press, Boston, 1966.
Barbour, Alan. *Humphrey Bogart*. Pyramid Books, New York, 1973.
Baxter, John. *Hollywood in the Thirties*. A.S. Barnes, New York, 1968.
Bergman, Andrew. *James Cagney*. Pyramid Books, New York, 1973.
————————. *We're in the Money*. New York University Press, New York, 1971.
Ferguson, Otis. *The Film Criticism of Otis Ferguson*. Temple University Press, 1971.
Haskell, Molly. *From Reverence to Rape: The Treatment of Women in the Movies*. Holt, Rinehart, and Winston, New York, 1974.
Higham, Charles, and Joei Greenberg. *Hollywood in the Forties*. A.S. Barnes, New York, 1968.
Langner, Lawrence. *The Magic Curtain*. E.P. Dutton & Co., New York, 1951.
LeRoy, Mervyn, with Dick Kleiner. *Take One*. Hawthorn, New York, 1974.
McCarty, Clifford. *Bogey: The Films of Humphrey Bogart*. Citadel Press, New York, 1965.
Parish, James Robert and Alvin H. Marill. *The Cinema of Edward G. Robinson*. A.S. Barnes, New York, 1972.
Robinson, Edward G., with Leonard Spigelgass. *All My Yesterdays*. Hawthorn, New York, 1973.
Robinson, Edward G., Jr., with William Duffy. *My Father, My Son*. Frederick Fell, New York, 1958.
Sennett, Ted. *Warner Brothers Presents*. Arlington House, New Rochelle, 1971.
Waldau, Roy S. *Vintage Years of the Theatre Guild*. Case Western Reserve University Press, Cleveland and London, 1972.
Warner, Jack and Dean Jennings. *My First One Hundred Years in Hollywood*. Random House, New York, 1965.
Warshow, Robert. *The Immediate Experience*. Doubleday & Co., Garden City, New York, 1962.

THE FILMS OF EDWARD G. ROBINSON

The director's name follows the release date. A (c) following the release date indicates that the film was in color. Sp indicates Screenplay and b/o indicates based/on.

1. THE BRIGHT SHAWL. First National, 1923. *John S. Robertson*. Sp: Edmund Goulding, b/o novel by Joseph Hergesheimer. Cast: Richard Barthelmess, Dorothy Gish, Jetta Goudal, William Powell, Mary Astor. Silent.

2. THE HOLE IN THE WALL. Paramount, 1929. *Robert Florey*. Sp: Pierre Collings, b/o play by Fred Jackson. Cast: Claudette Colbert, Donald Meek, Louise Closser Hale, Nelly Savage.

3. NIGHT RIDE. Universal, 1929. *John S. Robertson*. Sp: Edward T. Lowe, b/o story by Henry La Cossitt. Cast: Joseph Schildkraut, Barbara Kent, Harry Stubbs.

4. A LADY TO LOVE. MGM, 1930. *Victor Seastrom*. Sp: Sidney Howard, b/o his play, *They Knew What They Wanted*. Cast: Vilma Banky, Robert Ames, Richard Carle. Remade in 1940 under the play's title.

5. OUTSIDE THE LAW. Universal, 1930. *Tod Browning*. Sp: Browning and Garrett Fort. Cast: Mary Nolan, Owen Moore, Edwin Sturgis. Also filmed in 1921.

6. EAST IS WEST. Universal, 1930. *Monta Bell*. Sp: Winifred Eaton Reeve and Tom Reed, b/o play by Samuel Shipman and John Hymer. Cast: Lupe Velez, Lew Ayres, Tetsu Komai, Mary Forbes. Also filmed in 1922.

7. THE WIDOW FROM CHICAGO. First National, 1930. *Edward Cline*. Sp: Earl Baldwin. Cast: Alice White, Neil Hamilton, Frank McHugh, Lee Shumway.

8. LITTLE CAESAR. First National, 1931. *Mervyn LeRoy*. Sp: Francis E. Faragoh, b/o novel by W.R. Burnett. Cast: Douglas Fairbanks, Jr., Glenda Farrell, Sidney Blackmer, Ralph Ince, George E. Stone.

9. SMART MONEY. Warner Bros., 1931. *Alfred E. Green*. Sp: Kubec Glasmon, John Bright, Lucien Hubbard and Joseph Jackson. Cast: James Cagney, Evalyn Knapp, Boris Karloff, Noel Francis, Morgan Wallace.

10. FIVE STAR FINAL. First National, 1931. *Mervyn LeRoy*. Sp: Byron Morgan, b/o play by Louis Weitzenkorn. Cast: H.B. Warner, Marion Marsh, Ona Munson, Aline MacMahon, Boris Karloff, Gladys Lloyd.

11. THE HATCHET MAN. First National, 1932. *William A. Wellman*. Sp: J. Grubb Alexander, b/o play *The Honorable Mr. Wong* by Achmed Abdullah and David Belasco. Cast: Loretta Young, Dudley Digges, Leslie Fenton, Edmund Breese.

12. TWO SECONDS. First National, 1932. *Mervyn LeRoy*. Sp: Harvey Thew, b/o play by Elliott Lester. Cast: Preston Foster, Vivienne Osborne, J. Carrol Naish, Guy Kibbee.

13. TIGER SHARK. First National, 1932. *Howard Hawks*. Sp: Wells Root, b/o story "Tuna" by Houston Branch. Cast: Zita Johann, Richard Arlen, Leila Bennett, J. Carrol Naish.

14. SILVER DOLLAR. First National, 1932. *Alfred E. Green*. Sp: Carl Erickson and Harvey Thew, b/o biography by David Karsner. Cast: Bebe Daniels, Aline MacMahon, Jobyna Howland, DeWitt Jennings.

15. THE LITTLE GIANT. First National, 1933. *Roy Del Ruth*. Sp: Robert Lord and Wilson Mizner, b/o story by Robert Lord. Cast: Helen Vinson, Mary Astor, Kenneth Thomson, Shirley Grey, Berton Churchhill.

16. I LOVED A WOMAN. First National, 1933. *Alfred E. Green*. Sp: Charles Kenyon and Sidney Sutherland, b/o book by David Karsner. Cast: Kay Francis, Genevieve Tobin, J. Farrell MacDonald, Henry Kolker.

17. DARK HAZARD. First National, 1934. *Alfred E. Green*. Sp: Ralph Block and Brown Holmes, b/o novel by W.R. Burnett. Cast: Genevieve Tobin, Glenda Farrell, Gordon Westcott.

18. THE MAN WITH TWO FACES. First National, 1934. *Archie Mayo*. Sp: Tom Reed and Niven Busch, b/o play *The Dark Tower* by George S. Kaufman and Alexander Woollcott. Cast: Mary Astor, Ricardo Cortez, Louis Calhern, John Eldredge.

19. THE WHOLE TOWN'S TALKING. Columbia, 1935. *John Ford*. Sp: Jo Swerling and Robert Riskin, b/o novel by W.R. Burnett. Cast: Jean Arthur, Wallace Ford, Donald Meek, Ed Brophy.

20. BARBARY COAST. A Samuel Goldwyn Production, released by United Artists, 1935. *Howard Hawks.* Sp: Ben Hecht and Charles MacArthur. Cast: Miriam Hopkins, Joel McCrea, Walter Brennan, Frank Craven, Brian Donlevy.

21. BULLETS OR BALLOTS. First National, 1936. *William Keighley.* Sp: Seton I. Miller, b/o story by Miller and Martin Mooney. Cast: Joan Blondell, Barton MacLane, Humphrey Bogart, Frank McHugh, Joseph King.

22. KID GALAHAD. Warner Bros., 1937. *Michael Curtiz.* Sp: Seton I. Miller, b/o novel by Francis Wallace. Cast: Bette Davis, Wayne Morris, Jane Bryan, Humphrey Bogart, Veda Ann Borg. Remade in 1963.

23. THUNDER IN THE CITY. Columbia, 1937. *Marion Gering.* Sp: Robert Sherwood and Aben Kandel. Cast: Luli Deste, Nigel Bruce, Constance Collier, Ralph Richardson.

24. THE LAST GANGSTER. MGM, 1937. *Edward Ludwig.* Sp: John Lee Mahin, b/o story by William A. Wellman and Robert Carson. Cast: James Stewart, Rose Stradner, Lionel Stander, John Carradine, Grant Mitchell, Louise Beavers.

25. A SLIGHT CASE OF MURDER. Warner Bros., 1938. *Lloyd Bacon.* Sp: Earl Baldwin and Joseph Schrank, b/o play by Damon Runyon and Howard Lindsay. Cast: Jane Bryan, Ruth Donnelly, Willard Parker, Allen Jenkins. Remade in 1952 as *Stop, You're Killing Me*.

26. THE AMAZING DR. CLITTERHOUSE. Warner Bros., 1938. *Anatole Litvak.* Sp: John Wexley and John Huston, b/o play by Barré Lyndon. Cast: Claire Trevor, Gale Page, Donald Crisp, Humphrey Bogart, Thurston Hall, Vladimir Sokoloff, Henry O'Neill.

27. I AM THE LAW. Columbia, 1938. *Alexander Hall.* Sp: Jo Swerling, b/o stories by Fred Allhoff. Cast: Barbara O'Neil, John Beal, Wendy Barrie, Otto Kruger.

28. CONFESSIONS OF A NAZI SPY. Warner Bros., 1939. Anatole Litvak. Sp: Milton Krims and John Wexley, b/o *The Nazi Spy Conspiracy in America* by Leon G. Turrou. Cast: Francis Lederer, George Sanders, Paul Lukas, Lya Lys, Sig Rumann.

29. BLACKMAIL. MGM, 1939. *H.C. Potter.* Sp: David Hertz and William Ludwig. Cast: Ruth Hussey, Gene Lockhart, Bobs Watson, Guinn Williams.

30. DR. EHRLICH'S MAGIC BULLET. Warner Bros., 1940. *William Dieterle.* Sp: John Huston, Heinz Herald and Norman Burnside. Cast: Ruth Gordon, Otto Kruger, Donald Crisp, Sig Rumann, Maria Ouspenskaya.

31. BROTHER ORCHID. Warner Bros., 1940. *Lloyd Bacon*. Sp: Earl Baldwin, b/o story by Richard Connell. Cast: Ann Sothern, Ralph Bellamy, Humphrey Bogart, Donald Crisp, Allen Jenkins, Cecil Kellaway.

32. A DISPATCH FROM REUTERS. Warner Bros., 1940. *William Dieterle*. Sp: Milton Krims, b/o story by Valentine Williams and Wolfgang Wilhelm. Cast: Edna Best, Eddie Albert, Albert Basserman, Gene Lockhart.

33. THE SEA WOLF. Warner Bros., 1941. *Michael Curtiz*. Sp: Robert Rossen, b/o novel by Jack London. Cast: John Garfield, Ida Lupino, Alexander Knox, Gene Lockhart, Barry Fitzgerald. Also filmed in 1913, 1920, 1926 and 1930. Remade in 1958 as *Wolf Larsen*.

34. MANPOWER. Warner Bros., 1941. *Raoul Walsh*. Sp: Richard Macaulay and Jerry Wald. Cast: Marlene Dietrich, George Raft, Eve Arden, Alan Hale, Frank McHugh.

35. UNHOLY PARTNERS. MGM, 1941. *Mervyn LeRoy*. Sp: Earl Baldwin, Bartlett Cormack and Lesser Samuels. Cast: Laraine Day, Marsha Hunt, Edward Arnold, Charles Dingle.

36. LARCENY, INC. Warner Bros., 1942. Lloyd Bacon. Sp: Everett Freeman and Edwin Gilbert, b/o play *The Night Before Christmas* by Laura and S.J. Perelman. Cast: Jane Wyman, Broderick Crawford, Jack Carson, Anthony Quinn, Jackie Gleason.

37. TALES OF MANHATTAN. Twentieth-Century Fox, 1942. *Julien Duvivier*. Sp: Ben Hecht, Ferenc Molnar, Donald Ogden Stewart, Alan Campbell, Ladislas Fodor, Lamar Trotti. Cast (in Robinson sequence): George Sanders, James Gleason, Morris Ankrum, Mae Marsh.

38. DESTROYER. Columbia, 1943. *William A. Seiter*. Sp: Frank Wead, Lewis Meltzer and Borden Chase. Cast: Glenn Ford, Marguerite Chapman, Edgar Buchanan, Leo Gorcey, Regis Toomey, Larry Parks.

39. FLESH AND FANTASY (Episode 2). Universal, 1943. *Julien Duvivier*. Sp: Ernest Pascal, Samuel Hoffenstein and Ellis St. Joseph, b/o *Lord Arthur Saville's Crime* by Oscar Wilde. Cast: Charles Boyer, Thomas Mitchell, Anna Lee, Dame May Whitty.

40. TAMPICO. 20th Century-Fox. *Lothar Mendes*. Sp: Kenneth Gamet, Fred Niblo Jr. and Richard Macaulay, b/o story by Ladislas Fodor. Cast: Lynn Bari, Victor McLaglen, Mona Maris, Marc Lawrence.

41. MR. WINKLE GOES TO WAR. Columbia, 1944. *Alfred E. Green*. Sp: Waldo Salt, George Corey and Louis Solomon, b/o novel by Theodore Pratt. Cast: Ruth Warrick, Ted Donaldson, Bob Haymes.

42. DOUBLE INDEMNITY. Paramount, 1944. *Billy Wilder*. Sp: Wilder and Raymond Chandler, b/o novel by James M. Cain. Cast: Barbara Stanwyck, Fred MacMurray, Porter Hall, Tom Powers, Jean Heather.

43. THE WOMAN IN THE WINDOW. RKO, 1945. *Fritz Lang*. Sp: Nunnally Johnson, b/o novel *Once Off Guard* by J.H. Wallis. Cast: Raymond Massey, Joan Bennett, Dan Duryea, Edmond Breon.

44. OUR VINES HAVE TENDER GRAPES. MGM, 1945. *Roy Rowland*. Sp: Dalton Trumbo, b/o novel by George Victor Martin. Cast: Margaret O'Brien, Agnes Moorehead, James Craig, Morris Carnovsky, Frances Gifford, Jackie (Butch) Jenkins.

45. SCARLET STREET. Universal, 1946. *Fritz Lang*. Sp: Dudley Nichols, b/o novel and play *La Chienne* by Georges de la Fourcharliere. Cast: Joan Bennett, Dan Duryea, Margaret Lindsay, Rosalind Ivan.

46. JOURNEY TOGETHER. English Films, 1946. *John Boulting*. Sp: Terence Rattigan. Cast: Richard Attenborough, Jack Watling, David Tomlinson, Bessie Love.

47. THE STRANGER. RKO, 1946. *Orson Welles*. Sp: Anthony Veiller, John Huston and Welles, b/o story by Victor Trivas and Decla Dunning. Cast: Loretta Young, Orson Welles, Richard Long, Philip Merivale, Billy House.

48. THE RED HOUSE. A Sol Lesser Production, released by United Artists, 1947. *Delmer Daves*. Sp: Daves, b/o novel by George Agnew Chamberlain. Cast: Lon McCallister, Judith Anderson, Julie London, Rory Calhoun, Ona Munson.

49. ALL MY SONS. Universal, 1948. *Irving Reis*. Sp: Chester Erskine, b/o play by Arthur Miller. Cast: Burt Lancaster, Mady Christians, Louisa Horton, Howard Duff, Arlene Francis.

50. KEY LARGO. Warner Bros., 1948. *John Huston*. Sp: Richard Brooks and Huston, b/o play by Maxwell Anderson. Cast: Lauren Bacall, Humphrey Bogart, Claire Trevor, Lionel Barrymore, Thomas Gomez, Harry Lewis.

51. NIGHT HAS A THOUSAND EYES. Paramount, 1948. *John Farrow*. Sp: Barré Lyndon and Jonathan Latimer, b/o novel by Cornell Woolrich. Cast: Gail Russell, John Lund, Virginia Bruce, William Demarest.

52. HOUSE OF STRANGERS. 20th Century-Fox, 1949. *Joseph L. Mankiewicz*. Sp: Philip Yordan, b/o novel by Jerome Weidman. Cast: Richard Conte, Susan Hayward, Luther Adler, Debra Paget. Remade in 1954 as *Broken Lance*.

53. IT'S A GREAT FEELING. Warner Bros., 1949. *David Butler*. Sp: Jack Rose and Melville Shavelson, b/o story by I.A. L. Diamond. Cast: Dennis Morgan, Jack Carson, Doris Day, Bill Goodwin, many Warners guest stars.

54. MY DAUGHTER JOY (U.S. title: OPERATION X). Columbia, 1950. *Gregory Ratoff*. Sp: Robert Thoeren and William Rose, b/o novel *David Golder* by Irene Nemirowsky. Cast: Nora Swinburne, Peggy Cummins, Richard Greene, Finlay Currie, Gregory Ratoff.

55. ACTORS AND SIN (Segment: ACTOR'S BLOOD). United Artists, 1952. *Ben Hecht*. Sp: Hecht. Cast: Marsha Hunt, Dan O'Herlihy, Rudolph Anders.

56. VICE SQUAD. A Jules V. Levy-Arthur Gardner Production, released by United Artists, 1953. *Arnold Laven*. Sp: Lawrence Roman, b/o novel *Harness Bull* by Leslie T. White. Cast: Paulette Goddard, K.T. Stevens, Porter Hall, Joan Vohs, Lee Van Cleef.

57. BIG LEAGUER. MGM, 1953. *Robert Aldrich*. Sp: Herbert Baker, b/o story by John McNulty and Louis Morheim. Cast: Vera-Ellen, Jeff Richards, Richard Jaeckel.

58. THE GLASS WEB. Universal, 1953. *Jack Arnold*. Sp: Robert Blees and Leonard Lee, b/o novel by Max S. Ehrlich. Cast: John Forsythe, Marcia Henderson, Kathleen Hughes, Richard Denning.

59. BLACK TUESDAY. United Artists, 1954. *Hugo Fregonese*. Sp: Sidney Boehm. Cast: Peter Graves, Jean Parker, Warren Stevens, Milburn Stone.

60. THE VIOLENT MEN. Columbia, 1955 (c). *Rudolph Mate*. Sp: Harry Kleiner, b/o novel by Donald Hamilton. Cast: Glenn Ford, Barbara Stanwyck, Dianne Foster, Brian Keith, May Wynn, Lita Milan.

61. TIGHT SPOT. Columbia, 1955. *Phil Karlson*. Sp: William Bowers, b/o play *Dead Pigeon* by Lenard Kantor. Cast: Ginger Rogers, Brian Keith, Lorne Greene, Kathryn Grant.

62. A BULLET FOR JOEY. A Samuel Bischoff-David Diamond Production, released by United Artists, 1955. *Lewis Allen*. Sp: Geoffrey Homes and A.I. Bezzerides. Cast: George Raft, Audrey Totter, Peter Van Eyck, George Dolenz.

63. ILLEGAL. Warner Bros., 1955. *Lewis Allen*. Sp: W.R. Burnett and James R. Webb, b/o play *The Mouthpiece* by Frank J. Collins. Cast: Nina Foch, Jayne Mansfield, Hugh Marlowe, Albert Dekker. A remake of *The Mouthpiece* (1932).

64. HELL ON FRISCO BAY. Warner Bros., 1955 (c). *Frank Tuttle*. Sp: Sydney Boehm and Martin Rackin, b/o novel by William P. McGivern. Cast: Alan Ladd, Joanne Dru, Fay Wray, William Demarest, Paul Stewart.

65. NIGHTMARE. A Pine-Thomas-Shane Production, released by United Artists, 1956. *Maxwell Shane*. Sp: Shane, b/o novel by Cornell Woolrich. Cast: Kevin McCarthy, Connie Russell, Virginia Christine, Rhys Williams, Marian Carr.

66. THE TEN COMMANDMENTS. Paramount, 1956 (c). *Cecil B. DeMille*. Sp: Aeneas MacKenzie, Jesse L. Lasky Jr., Jack Gariss, and Frederic M. Frank, b/o novels *Prince of Egypt* by Dorothy Clarke Wilson, *Pillar of Fire* by Rev. J. H. Ingraham, *On Eagle's Wings* by Rev. G. E. Southon, in accordance with The Holy Scripture. Cast: Charlton Heston, Yul Brynner, Anne Baxter, Yvonne DeCarlo, Debra Paget, John Derek, Sir Cedric Hardwicke, Nina Foch, Martha Scott, Judith Anderson, Vincent Price, John Carradine.

67. A HOLE IN THE HEAD. A Sincap Production, released by United Artists, 1959 (c). *Frank Capra*. Sp: Arnold Schulman, b/o his play. Cast: Frank Sinatra, Eleanor Parker, Thelma Ritter, Eddie Hodges, Carolyn Jones.

68. PEPE. Columbia, 1969 (c). *George Sidney*. Sp: Dorothy Kingsley and Claude Binyon. Cast: Cantinflas, Dan Dailey, Shirley Jones, Carlos Montalban, many guest stars.

69. SEVEN THIEVES. 20th Century-Fox, 1960. *Henry Hathaway*. Sp: Sydney Boehm, b/o novel *Lions at the Kill* by Max Catto. Cast: Rod Steiger, Joan Collins, Eli Wallach, Alexander Scourby, Sebastian Cabot.

70. MY GEISHA. Paramount, 1961 (c). *Jack Cardiff*. Sp: Norman Krasna. Cast: Shirley MacLaine, Yves Montand, Bob Cummings.

71. TWO WEEKS IN ANOTHER TOWN. MGM, 1962 (c). *Vincente Minnelli*. Sp: Charles Schnee, b/o novel by Irwin Shaw. Cast: Kirk Douglas, Cyd Charisse, George Hamilton, Dahlia Lavi, Claire Trevor, Rosanna Schiaffino.

72. THE PRIZE. MGM, 1964 (c). *Mark Robson*. Sp: Ernest Lehman, b/o novel by Irving Wallace. Cast: Paul Newman, Elke Sommer, Diane Baker, Micheline Presle, Sergio Fantoni.

73. GOOD NEIGHBOR SAM. Columbia, 1964 (c). *David Swift*. Sp: James Fritzell, Everett Greenbaum and Swift, b/o novel by Jack Finney. Cast: Jack Lemmon, Romy Schneider, Dorothy Provine, Michael Connors.

74. ROBIN AND THE SEVEN HOODS. Warner Bros., 1964 (c). *Gordon Douglas*. Sp: David R. Schwartz. Cast: Frank Sinatra, Dean Martin, Bing Crosby, Barbara Rush, Peter Falk, Sammy Davis, Jr.

75. THE OUTRAGE. MGM, 1964. *Martin Ritt*. Sp: Michael Kanin, b/o film *Rashomon*, stories by Ryunosuke Akutagawa and play *Rashomon* by Fay and Michael Kanin. Cast: Paul Newman, Laurence Harvey, Claire Bloom, William Shatner, Howard da Silva.

76. CHEYENNE AUTUMN. Warner Bros., 1964 (c). *John Ford*. Sp: James R. Webb, suggested by the novel *Cheyenne Autumn* by Mari Sandoz. Cast: Carroll Baker, Richard Widmark, Karl Malden, James Stewart, Dolores Del Rio, Arthur Kennedy, Sal Mineo, Ricardo Montalban.

77. A BOY TEN FEET TALL. Paramount, 1965 (c). *Alexander Mackendrick*. Sp: Denis Cannan, b/o novel *Sammy Going South* by W.H. Canaway. Cast: Fergus McClelland, Constance Cummings, Harry H. Corbett.

78. THE CINCINNATI KID. MGM, 1965 (c). *Norman Jewison*. Sp: Ring Lardner, Jr. and Terry Southern, b/o novel by Richard Jessup. Cast: Steve McQueen, Tuesday Weld, Ann-Margret, Karl Malden, Rip Torn, Joan Blondell.

79. THE BLONDE FROM PEKING. Paramount, 1968 (c). *Nicolas Gessner*. Sp: Gessner and Mark Behm. Cast: Mireille Darc, Giorgia Moll, Claudio Brook.

80. THE BIGGEST BUNDLE OF THEM ALL. MGM, 1968 (c). *Ken Annakin*. Sp: Sy Salkowitz. Cast: Raquel Welch, Robert Wagner, Vittorio De Sica, Godfrey Cambridge.

81. GRAND SLAM. Paramount, 1968 (c). *Giuliano Montaldo*. Sp: Mino Roli, Caminito, Marcello Fondato, Antonio De La Loma and Marcello Coscia. Cast: Janet Leigh, Adolpho Celi, George Rigaud, Klaus Kinski.

82. UNO SCACCO TUTTO MATTO. Kinesis Films/Miniter/Tecisa, 1968 (c). *Robert Fiz*. Sp: Fiz, Massimilliano Capriccoli, Ennio De Concini, Joe G. Maesso, Leonardo Martin, Juan Cesarabea. Cast: Terry-Thomas, Maria Grazia Buccella, Adolfo Celi.

83. OPERATION ST. PETER'S. Paramount, 1968 (c). *Lucio Fulci*. Sp: Ennio De Concini, Adriano Baracco, Roberto Gianviti and Signor Fulci. Cast: Lando Buzzanca, Heinz Ruhmann, Jean-Claude Biraly, Uta Levka.

84. NEVER A DULL MOMENT. Buena Vista, 1968 (c). *Jerry Paris*. Sp: A.J. Carothers, b/o novel by John Godey. Cast: Dick Van Dyke, Dorothy Provine, Henry Silva, Joanna Moore, Tony Bill, Slim Pickens, Jack Elam.

85. MACKENNA'S GOLD. Columbia, 1969 (c). *J. Lee Thompson*. Sp: Carl Foreman, b/o novel by Will Henry. Cast: Gregory Peck, Omar Sharif, Telly Savalas, Camilla Sparv, Julie Newmar, Lee J. Cobb, Raymond Massey.

86. SONG OF NORWAY. Cinerama, 1970 (c). *Andrew L. Stone*. Sp: Stone, suggested by play by Milton Lazarus, Robert Wright and George Forrest, from a play by Homer Curran. Cast: Toralv Maurstad, Florence Henderson, Christina Schollin, Frank Poretta, Harry Secombe, Robert Morley, Oscar Homolka.

87. SOYLENT GREEN. MGM, 1973. *Richard Fleischer*. Sp: Stanley R. Greenberg, b/o novel *Make Room, Make Room* by Harry Harrison. Cast: Charlton Heston, Leigh Taylor-Young, Chuck Connors, Joseph Cotten.

INDEX

Actors and Sin, 109
All My Sons, 64, 67, 84, 90-93, 105, 140
Amazing Dr. Clitterhouse, The, 60, 134
Androcles and the Lion, 19, 20
Ann-Margret, 139
Arlen, Richard, 42
Arliss, George, 20

Bacall, Lauren, 83
Banky, Vilma, 24
Barbary Coast, 32, 45, 48
Barnes, Howard, 73
Barrymore, Ethel, 18
Barrymore, Lionel, 83
Ben-Ami, Jacob, 18
Bennett, Joan, 87, 89
Big Leaguer, The, 108
Biggest Bundle of Them All, The, 122
Black Tuesday, 109
Blackmail, 53
Blondell, Joan, 139
Bogart, Humphrey, 13, 15, 47
Boy Ten Feet Tall, A, 126
Brecht, Bertolt, 141
Brooks, Richard, 83
Brother Orchid, 69, 98
Bryan, Jane, 47
Bullet for Joey, A, 112, 116-117
Bullets or Ballots, 53, 57-60, 62, 73
Burnett, W.R., 29, 78

Cagney, James, 13, 15, 35, 37, 48
Cain, James M., 94
Capone, Al, 15, 20, 32
Capra, Frank, 120
Chandler, Raymond, 94
Chaney, Lon, 20
Chayefsky, Paddy, 119, 120
Chekhov, Anton, 141
Cheyenne Autumn, 134

Cincinnati Kid, The, 134, 137, 139
Colman, Ronald, 24
Confessions of a Nazi Spy, 62-63, 96
Crowther, Bosley, 53, 83, 94, 101
Curtiz, Michael, 48, 78

Dark Hazard, 50
Darkness at Noon, 106, 108
Davis, Bette, 48
Day, Doris, 105
Death of a Salesman, 90, 93
Deluge, The, 18
DeMille, Cecil B., 117
Destroyer, 99
Dieterle, William
Deitrich, Marlene, 103, 104
Dispatch from Reuters, A, 69
Dr. Ehrlich's Magic Bullet, 44, 64, 67, 69-70, 73, 76, 84
Donnelly, Ruth, 50
Dostoyevsky, Fydor, 19
Double Indemnity, 64, 67, 69, 94, 109
Douglas, Kirk, 132
Dragnet, 112
Duryea, Dan, 89, 90

East is West, 24

Fairbanks, Jr., Douglas, 27
Farrell, Glenda, 28
Ferguson, Otis, 73
Five Star Final, 32, 39
Flesh and Fantasy, 99
Ford, John, 48, 50, 134
Foster, Preston, 42
Front Page, The, 40

Glass Web, The, 109
Gleason, Jackie, 134
Goat Song, 19

155

Goddard, Paulette, 114
Good Neighbor Sam, 126
Gordon, Ruth, 70
Grand Slam, 122

Hardwicke, Cedric, 60
Hatchet Man, The, 32, 35
Hawks, Howard, 42, 45
Hecht, Ben, 39, 45, 109
Hell on Frisco Bay, 108, 109, 111, 117
Hole in the Head, A, 120-121
Hole in the Wall, The, 23
Hopkins, Arthur, 20
Hopkins, Miriam, 45
House of Strangers, 64, 93, 105
Howard, Sidney, 19, 23
Hustler, The, 134
Huston, John, 81, 83

I Am the Law, 62
I Loved a Woman, 50
Ibsen, Henrik, 141
Idol, The, 35
Illegal, 109, 112
It's a Great Feeling, 105

Jewison, Norman, 134
Johann, Zita, 40
Juarez and Maximilian, 19

Keith Brian, 109
Key Largo, 64, 67, 69, 78, 81-84, 105, 116, 117, 134
Kibitzer, The, 20
Kid Galahad, 32, 45, 47-48, 73
Knox, Alexander, 80
Koestler, Arthur, 108
Komisarjevsky, 20

Ladd, Alan, 109

Lady to Love, A, 23-24, 40
Lancaster, Burt, 90
Lang, Fritz, 64, 67, 84
Larceny, Inc., 98
Last Gangster, The, 48
Laughton, Charles, 23
LeRoy, Mervyn, 27, 31, 42, 43
Life of Emile Zola, The, 69
Little Caesar, 11, 15, 23, 24, 26, 27-32, 42, 44, 48, 50, 53, 73, 78, 141
Little Giant, 48, 50, 53
Little Teacher, The, 18
Lombard, Carol, 23
London, Jack, 78
Lord, Pauline, 20
Lukas, Paul, 63
Lunts, The, 20
Lupino, Ida, 80

MacArthur, Charles, 40, 45
Mackenna's Gold, 126
MacMahon, Aline, 39
MacMurray, Fred, 94
Man with Red Hair, The, 20
Man with Two Faces, The, 62, 109
Manpower, 101, 103-104
McCrea, Joel, 45
McQueen, Steve, 137, 139
Melville, Herman, 80
Middle of the Night, 119-120
Miller, Arthur, 90, 93
Minnelli, Vincente, 134
Moby Dick, 80
Moorehead, Agnes, 73, 96
Morris, Wayne, 47
Mr. Samuel, 23
Mr. Winkle Goes to War, 99, 101
Muni, Paul, 69
My Geisha, 126

Ned McCobb's Daughter, 19
Never a Dull Moment, 122
Night Has a Thousand Eyes, 99
Night Ride, 24
Nugent, Frank, 60, 63

O-Brien, Margaret, 73, 74, 76
Osborne, Vivienne, 42
Our Vines Have Tender Grapes, 64, 67, 69, 73-74, 76, 84
Outrage, The, 126, 128
Outside the Law, 24

Pawn, The, 18
Pirandello, Luigi, 19
Pollack, Arthur, 23
Price, The, 90
Prize, The, 126
Public Enemy, The, 27, 37, 48

Racket, The, 20
Raft, George, 101, 116, 117
Rains, Claude, 106
Rashomon, 128, 130
Rathburn, Stephen, 20
Red Channels, 105
Red House, The, 98
Reis Irving, 93
Right You Are, 19
Ritt, Martin, 128
Ritter, Thelma, 120, 121
Robin and the Seven Hoods, 122
Robin, Leo, 69
Rogers, Ginger, 109
Ruhl, Arthur, 20
Runyon, Damon, 49, 120

Sanders, George, 63
Scarface, 27
Scarlet Street, 64, 84, 89-90, 93

Schildkraut, Joseph, 20
Sea Wolf, The, 64, 67, 69, 78-81, 84, 140
Seven Thieves, 122, 123
Shaw, George Bernard, 19
Silver Dollar, 32
Sinatra, Frank, 120
Skolsky, Sidney, 15
Slight Case of Murder, A, 32, 48, 49-50, 78
Smart Money, 32, 35, 37, 39, 78
Song of Norway, 126
Soylent Green, 126
Stanwyck, Barbara, 94, 109
Steiger, Rod, 123
Story of Louis Pasteur, The, 69
Stranger, The, 94, 96-98
Sunset Boulevard, 130
Swerling, Jo, 20

Tales of Manhattan, 99
Tampico, 99
Ten Commandments, The, 117-119
Thunder in the City, 50
Tiger Shark, 35, 40, 42, 101
Tight Spot, 109, 112
Tracy, Spencer, 134
Trevor, Claire, 83, 132, 134
Two Seconds, 32, 42-44
Two Weeks in Another Town, 126, 130, 132-134

Under Fire, 18
Unholy Partners, 98

Vice Squad, 108, 112, 120
Violent Men, The, 109

Wallach, Eli, 123
Walsh, Raoul, 101
Welch, Raquel, 122
Weld, Tuesday, 139

Welles, Orson, 94, 96, 98
Werfel, Franz, 19
White, Alice, 25
Whole Town's Talking, The, 44, 48-49, 89
Widow from Chicago, The, 25
Wilder, Billy, 94
Woman in the Window, 64, 84-87, 89, 90, 140

Woollcott, Alexander, 20
Wray, Fay, 109

Young, Loretta, 96, 98

Zimmerman, Paul, 126
Zinsser, William, 111

ABOUT THE AUTHOR

Foster Hirsch has written for numerous publications including *The New Republic, The Nation, Commonweal, America, Variety, The New York Times, The Village Voice, Film Quarterly, Film Heritage, Cinema, Take One, Crawdaddy, Fusion, Kansas Quarterly, Judaism, The Educational Theatre Journal, Arts in Society,* and *Shakespeare Quarterly*. He has contributed essays to several film and drama anthologies, and he has written books on George Kelly, Tennessee Williams, and (for the Pyramid Illustrated History of the Movies) Elizabeth Taylor. He is currently at work on a book on the epic film. He is Assistant Professor of English and Film at Brooklyn College.

ABOUT THE EDITOR

Ted Sennett is the author of *Warner Brothers Presents*, a tribute to the great Warners films of the Thirties and Forties, and of *Lunatics and Lovers*, on the long-vanished but well-remembered "screwball" comedies of the past. He is also the editor of *The Movie Buff's Book* and has written about films for magazines and newspapers. He lives in New Jersey with his wife and three children.